ΔD Architectural Design

Home Front: New Developments in Housing

Guest-edited by Lucy Bullivant

⦿WILEY-ACADEMY

Architectural Design
Vol 73 No 4 July/August 2003

Editorial Offices
International House
Ealing Broadway Centre
London W5 5DB
T: +44 (0)20 8326 3800
F: +44 (0)20 8326 3801
E: architecturaldesign@wiley.co.uk

Editor
Helen Castle
Production
Mariangela Palazzi-Williams
Project Coordinator
Caroline Ellerby
Art Director
Christian Küsters ↘ CHK Design
Designer
Scott Bradley ↘ CHK Design
Picture Editor
Famida Rasheed

Advertisement Sales
01243 843272

Editorial Board
Denise Bratton, Adriaan Beukers,
André Chaszar, Peter Cook,
Max Fordham, Massimiliano
Fuksas, Edwin Heathcote,
Anthony Hunt, Charles Jencks,
Jan Kaplicky, Robert Maxwell,
Jayne Merkel, Monica Pidgeon,
Antoine Predock, Leon van Schaik

Contributing Editors
André Chaszar
Craig Kellogg
Jeremy Melvin
Jayne Merkel

ISBN 0-47084874-X
Profile No 164

Abbreviated positions
t=top, b=bottom, c=centre, l=left, r=right

Front cover: Pugh Scarpa Kodama Architects, Colorado Court, Santa Monica, California (realised 2002) © Pugh Scarpa Kodama
Back cover: BKK-3 Architektur, Miss Sargfabrik, Vienna (realised 1998) © Hertha Hurnaus

AD
pp 4-7 © Hertha Hurnaus; p 8 © Pugh Scarpa Kodama; p 9(bl) photo: Michael Mack; p 9 (tr&br) photos: Alex de Rijke; p 10 courtesy SocióPolis; pp 11 & 14 © West 8/Jeroen Musch; p 12 © NL Architects; pp 16 & 21 © Christian Richters; pp 18, 19(tl&r) & 20(tl&bl) © Architectenbureau Marlies Rohmer; pp 19(bl) & 20(tr&br) photos: Roos Aldershoff; p 22 © Urban Affairs, photos: Marco Vermeulen; p 23 portrait © Matt Wright, all other photography © Urban Splash; pp 24-6 © Urban Splash; pp 27-8 © Alsop Architects Ltd; pp 29-30 © Stephenson Bell Architects, photos: Charlotte Wood; p 35(t) photo: Raf Makda; p 35(b) photo: Larry Bray; pp 36-7 © George Wimpey City; pp 38-9 © Greenwich Millennium Village; pp 40 & 43(tr) © Haworth Tompkins Limited, photos: Phil Sayer; pp 42 & 43(c) © Haworth Tompkins Limited, photos: Philip Vile; p 43(tl) © Haworth Tompkins Limited; p 43(b) © Haworth Tompkins Limited, photos: Morley von Sternberg; p 46 (tl&tr) courtesy Sergison Bates Architects, photos: Ioana Marinescu; pp 46(b) & 47 courtesy Sergison Bates Architects; pp 48 & 49 (tr&b) © Proctor and Matthews Architects; p 49 model photography: Peter Bennett, models produced by Capital Models, London; pp 50-1 © BoKlok; p 52 courtesy Ola Nylander, photo: Jappe Ligedahl; pp 53-6 © Ola Nylander; pp 57, 58(br), 59, 60(t), 61-2 & 63(l) © Mark Prizeman; p 60(c&b) © Takuya Onishi; p 63 (r) © Paul Oliver from Dwellings: The Vernacular House published world-wide by Phaidon Press, London, 2003; pp 64-9 © Gans & Jelacic; pp 70 & 78(bl&br)) © Marpillero Pollak Architects; pp 72-3 © David Sundberg/ESTO;

p 74(tl&bl) courtesy Agrest and Gandelsonas; p 74 (r) courtesy Agrest and Gandelsonas photo: Aaron Forest; p 75(t&b) © Ohlhausen DuBois Architects; p 75(c) photo: Norman McGrath; p 76 courtesy Thanhauser Esterson Kapell Architects; p 77 (t) © Pasanella + Klein Stolzman + Berg Architects, P.C.; p 77(c&b) © Paul Warchol; pp 78(tl,tr,cl,&cr) © New York City Housing Authority; p 79 © Hanrahan + Meyers Architects; p 80 renderings and plans © Caples Jefferson Architects, model photos: Preston Photography; p 81 © Alexander Gorlin Architects; pp 82-3 photos: Toshi Kobayashi; p 84(l) photo: Akira Itoh; p 84(cl&cr) photos: Yasunori Shimomura; pp 84(r) & 85 photos: Shinkenchiku-sha; p 86 courtesy FOB Association; p 87 model photos: © C+A, building photos: Satoshi Asakawa; p 88 © Satoshi Minakawa; p 89(lx4) © Nacasa & Partners Inc.; p 89(t&cr) © Soichi Murazumi; p 90 © Hully Liveris, photo: Wayne Miles; p 91 © Patrick Bingham-Hall; p 92(l) © Shahreen Fantin; p 92(r) © Richard Stringer; p 93 © Peter Hyatt; p 94 © Lindsay Clare, photo: Richard Stringer; p 95(r) © Stanisic Associates / Turner Associates, photo: Brett Boardman; pp 96-7 courtesy Design Inc. Architects, Crown Copyright.

AD+
pp 100+, 101+ (r) & 102+ photos: © Catherine Tighe; p 101+(l) photo: James Wilson; pp 103+, 106+(t&br) & 107+ photos: © Guy Wenbourne; p 106+(bl) & 108+ photos: © Enrique Browne; pp 109-111+, 113+ & 115+ © Nigel Green; pp 112+ & 114+ © Duncan Lewis Scape Architecture; pp 116+ & 119+ images: Kristina Shea and Jeroen van Mechelen (EXP.architects, Amsterdam, NL); p 117+ images: Andrew Maher; p 118+(tl&bl) courtesy Dr Jeff Heisserman, Terabeam; p 118+(tr) courtesy Jay McCormack, Computational Design Lab, Department of Mechanical Engineering, Carnegie Mellon University; pp 120-1+ images: Kristina Shea; p 122+ © ADAGP, Paris and DACS, London 2003; p 124+ Reproduced by permission of English Heritage. NMR.

Subscription Offices UK
John Wiley & Sons Ltd.
Journals Administration Department
1 Oldlands Way, Bognor Regis
West Sussex, PO22 9SA
T: +44 (0)1243 843272
F: +44 (0)1243 843232
E: cs-journals@wiley.co.uk

Annual Subscription Rates 2003
Institutional Rate: UK £160
Personal Rate: UK £99
Student Rate: UK £70
Institutional Rate: US $240
Personal Rate: US $150
Student Rate: US $105
ᗐ is published bi-monthly.
Prices are for six issues and include postage and handling charges.
Periodicals postage paid at Jamaica, NY 11431. Air freight and mailing in the USA by Publications Expediting Services Inc, 200 Meacham Avenue, Elmont, NY 11003

Single Issues UK: £22.50
Single Issues outside UK: US $45.00
Details of postage and packing charges available on request

Postmaster
Send address changes to ᗐ Publications Expediting Services, 200 Meacham Avenue, Elmont, NY 11003

Printed in Italy. All prices are subject to change without notice. [ISSN: 0003-8504]

11
23
29
40
50
70
82
90
103+
109+
116+
122+
126+

Home Front: New Developments in Housing
Guest-edited by Lucy Bullivant

For *Architectural Design* in the 1950s and 1960s, housing was a mainstay. As Monica Pidgeon, the pioneering editor of $\triangle$ (1941–75), has told me, she was always certain to dedicate at least one or two issues a year to the subject. By the 1980s this situation had changed dramatically. Housing, it seemed, had dropped, not entirely voluntarily, off the architectural radar. If housing was published in $\triangle$, it was under the banner of a particular style rather than as a dedicated entity. This was a reflection of the times as much as $\triangle$'s new editorial direction. Privatisation and the perceived failure of Modernist public housing had placed architects, in the UK at least, at the periphery of housing procurement. Thatcherite legislation and policy privileged the hegemony of the market-led house builders with their catalogue of national house-types.

Fifteen years on, it seems architects are, with a new tenacity, making a quiet comeback. As Lucy Bullivant states in her Introduction, what this issue of $\triangle$ does so powerfully is argue for 'reimagining the terms of architecture's social engagement'. This has to be by necessity a far more creative, resourceful process than ever before. The task before them in housing means that architects are always working to tight restraints, whether physical — in terms of site, planning or economics — or in terms of the various parties they are required to satisfy within a multilayered process.

Rather than being a thorough survey, this title represents a series of snapshots into housing internationally. With each shift of geographical focus comes a shift in topic and onus. Thus new developments in housing are covered with no claim to a comprehensive treatment. These are as diverse as modular and prefabrication techniques, property development, planning, public space and emergency provision. In each situation the cultural, economic, social and political conditions create a unique blend, with the complexities of each context throwing up new problems, but also new solutions. Often our expectations of individual areas are confounded, as illustrated in this issue by the difficulties encountered in delivering architectural quality in the Netherlands and Sweden (both countries renowned for their social responsibility) and an enlightened scheme for community centres in New York. But what is common to most, if not all the regions featured in this issue, is that the plug was pulled on government funding of public housing in the 1980s.

Without any pretence that architects have recovered their old place in the housing sector, there is certainly now more scope for architectural solutions. This is certainly true whether architects are applying their skills to the spatial honing of high-density schemes, to the creation of bespoke designs that aid the sale of a private component in a mixed scheme or the development of new production and construction techniques. Housing is certainly back on the agenda as far as $\triangle$ is concerned. $\triangle$

Housing is about the supply of houses, while also being a prism through which housing policy and cultural currents in society can be viewed.

Today's urbanised world has to tackle the housing situation seriously and learn how to cope with enormous varieties of population in terms of socio-economic strata, cultural and ethnic differences, aspirations and access to the wealth of society. The situation in the UK, with the introduction in 2000 of PPG3, even suggests that land shortage and a requirement for higher densities might make the relationship between property development and housing design symbiotic.

Recognising how such mechanisms of change can be creatively drawn upon, avoiding standardised solutions and reimagining the terms of architecture's social engagement is a process that can be carried out only with the active involvement of all the parties responsible for housing procurement. The failure, nonexistence, of public housing, indeed its decimation at any level, needs to be combated by an embedding of intelligent strategies. These are inevitably concerned with the liminal space of public/private that is also a psychological space of interior/exterior worlds and the appropriation of old by new, and are instrumental through the forging of new identities for partnerships at every level.

In the face of retreat from investment in provision for public housing by governments across the world, for example in Sweden despite its pioneering history in this area (see Ola Nylander, 'The Swedish Home'), Australia (see Lindsay Johnston, 'ABBA Housing and Beyond') and in the UK (see Helen Castle's 'Profile of Tom

Bloxham of Urban Splash' and 'Interview with David Birkbeck of Design for Homes', and 'Mediating Thresholds Between Public and Private Space in UK Housing Design' by Rob Wilson) – all with differing results – a profound evaluation of the succeeding alternatives is essential.

In the shift to market-led solutions, new housing concepts relating to a variety of needs require strong alliances of developers, architects and agencies, and clear strategies for use, so the public/private solutions resulting do not suffer from tunnel vision. Developers and estate agents may now be more sociologically attuned to lifestyle concepts, yet pushing boundaries in design, technology and procurement needs to be matched by open-mindedness and creative risk on the part of more private developers.

In terms of sensitivity to the changing needs of housing provision, the role of the market is clearly largely curtailed by business-led rather than cultural projections. However, architects like FOBA (see Thomas Daniell, 'Architects as Housemakers is Japan') and developers such as Urban Splash in Manchester and Liverpool (see Helen Castle, 'Profile of Tom Bloxham') show that evolving new housing models that will be accepted can be carried out through integration of the mechanisms of business with architectural concepts. This offers the potential to be instinctive and pragmatic about realising a distinct bottom-up agenda for housing, upping the ante in the quality of social provision. In an era of major threat to affordable housing provision globally, the New York City Housing Authority's strategies demonstrate that public-housing provision can still be achieved at a high level

(see Jayne Merkel, 'Fine Tuning: How the New York City Housing Authority Makes Housing Work').

Emergency housing, addressed in this issue in two separate essays by Mark Prizeman, and Deborah Gans and Matthew Jelacic, is a galling example of how top-down paternalistic aid and its planning regimes export idealised Western values of lifestyle and cohesion. It sets its sights on an environmental context that needs a much more situated, localised set of strategies to put in train support systems appropriate in every case and adaptable to the change that is the constant of emergency situations.

The heartstrings of Western industrialised society are tugged back and forth by housing as a basic need, and in particular between simultaneous urges for individuality and communality as sources of happiness. The desire for exposure to new experiences has led not only to a preoccupation with changing the interior design of a house, but also to adaptability – right down to creating within it intelligent responsive systems – while houses themselves are still being built in rigid, uniform designs. If the infiltration of housing by market-led design values has changed the mindset of a generation, then the signs are that expectations are slowly spreading to the liminal spaces where private and public meet (see article by Rob Wilson).

Housing expectations could have a centrifugal impact at an urban scale, changing, through the reinvention of the space at one's front door,

perceptions of a more palpable relationship with the environment, as well as making 'sustainability' a lived reality at a microcosmic, communal level and not just an overused buzz word. But this can only result from teamwork. It has to be inclusive. It has to evolve in tandem with a reappraisal of the social contracts that create the access conditions to neighbourhoods and their housing provision. These are hardly democratically negotiated, except in countries such as the Netherlands, which is itself under pressure from market forces (see Lucy Bullivant, 'Working the Programme'). It is a country that has applied the twinning protocol to create sister-city relations, for example Rotterdam and Durban, and in South Africa through the Housing Generator project,[1] one feature of which is the mutual exposure to problems that are then addressed bilaterally.

Along with the more global dynamic of converging transnationally to address issues is the localised motivation to connect through housing not just the domestic interior and its exterior, but also culture and nature. By identifying the strands of connections between changing patterns in society and housing in particular, the significance of domestic design to industrialised societies is deepened. To those without a home, its significance has never been lessened as mobility has generally meant dispossession.

Such a prevalent and intense impulse to mediate and make real thresholds underlines the need to avoid focusing on universal solutions. Instead, as New York architects Deborah Gans and Matthew Jelacic advocate in this issue , the times in which we live demand that we 'situate the project in relation to recurring desires'.

Miss Sargfabrik, Vienna (realised 1998)
BKK-3 Architektur

Miss Sargfabrik is a cooperative-like complex of 40 apartment units with a total usable space of 3,000 square metres complemented by common areas of extraordinary architecture and constructed at a cost of 3.8 million. The complex won the Austrian Adolf Loos Architecture Prize and the Berlin Academy of Art's Kunstpreis 2002. It aims to satisfy hybrid human needs in the 21st century: dwelling, working, living, dreaming, togetherness instead of loneliness, individuality, community, experiencing space and zones of tranquillity. Franz Sumnitsch of BKK-3 calls these the challenges rather than the contradictions of a new breed of architecture.[2] He feels that while there are no end of fashionable buzz words to try to describe the 'life sentiment' of the 21st century, there have been few examples of its realisation. Even the smaller apartments of between 50 and 60 square metres have ceiling heights that can only be found in old buildings. Sloping floors and ceilings evoke the creativity of the dwellers.

The concept of Miss Sargfabrik incorporates memories of the Viennese tradition of social housing, as well as communitarian thinking that is now common knowledge. Architecturally, all boundaries merge and interweave, and thus create new qualities. The intention to create unfolding rather than bound space leads to an evolutionary architecture manifested in an architectural organism characterised by social diversity. The 40 units house a social commune run by the Vienna city administration, with some units for people in wheelchairs and small 'flex box' apartments let to students for a period of one year. Quality of life is not only the prerogative of the rich. All tenants live in the home of their own making, and their wishes regarding the design and the details of the architecture have been canvassed and then considered in all the apartments.

Colorado Court, Santa Monica, California (realised 2002)
Pugh Scarpa Kodama Architects

Colorado Court will be one of the first buildings of its type in the US that is totally energy independent. Architect Larry Scarpa of Pugh Scarpa also founded Liveable Places (www.liveableplaces.org), a non-profit organisation that creates sustainable affordable housing on problematic urban sites and aims to influence urban policy-makers and citizens in housing matters, and is a pioneer in the field of social housing projects.

Designed for the Community Corporation of Santa Monica, Colorado Court distinguishes itself from most conventionally developed projects in that it incorporates energy-efficient measures that exceed standard practice, optimise building performance and ensure reduced energy use during all phases of construction and occupancy. Its planning and design emerged from close consideration and employment of passive solar-design strategies that include: locating and orienting the building to control solar cooling loads; shaping and orienting the building for exposure to prevailing winds; shaping the building to induce buoyancy for natural ventilation; designing windows to maximise daylighting; shading south-facing windows and minimising west-facing glazing. The windows are designed to maximise natural ventilation, and the interiors are shaped and planned to enhance daylight and natural air-flow distribution.

The architects hope that the techniques and strategies developed in the project will inspire and provide a model for future development, while increasing awareness and instilling confidence and incentive in those public and private agencies and individuals responsible for the production of projects of this kind to strive for practices geared towards the preservation and improvement of the built environment.

Colorado Court features several state-of-the-art technologies that distinguish it as a model demonstration building of sustainable-energy supply and utilisation. These technologies include a natural-gas-powered turbine/heat-recovery system that will generate the base electrical load and hot-water demands for the building, and a solar-electric panel system integrated into the facade and roof of the building that will supply most of the peak-load electricity demand. The co-generation system will convert utility natural gas to electricity to meet the base-load power needs of the building and will capture waste heat to produce hot water for the building throughout the year as well as space heating needs in the winter. This system will have a conversion efficiency of natural gas in excess of 70 per cent compared to a less than 30 per cent conversion efficiency of primary energy delivered by the utility grid at the building site. The solar photovoltaic system will produce green electricity at the building site that releases no pollutants to the environment. The panels are integral to the building envelope and unused solar electricity will be delivered to the grid during the daytime and retrieved from the grid at night as needed. These systems will pay for themselves in less than 10 years and annual savings in electricity and natural-gas bills are estimated to be in excess of $6000.

Long fascinated by high-density housing as the archetypal urban mode, dRMM has studied four-storey apartment blocks in Europe, in particular recent Dutch examples. Consequently the architects have developed different organisation and access principles, and ideas for prefabricated material/construction tactics. The firm's recent work examines this typology in relation to changing lifestyle/plan patterns and the green construction agenda generally.

No. One Centaur Street, an apartment building situated less than 2 metres from the Eurostar viaduct, may seem unlikely but dRMM's commission was based on the idea of a new housing typology for brownfield sites in London,[3] a hybrid of the European horizontal apartment and the English vertical terraced house. Each apartment has a *Raumplan* interior organised as a large, open, double-height living space, interpenetrated by adjacent enclosed bedrooms and stairs that form a concrete buffer to the railway. Construction consists internally of high-quality exposed concrete, economically overclad externally with insulated rain screen. Other than in-situ concrete, all components are prefabricated, specified from international sources according to dRMM's catalogue design methodology.

SocióPolis, a project for social housing in the information era directed by the Spanish architect Vicente Guallart for the Generalitat Valenciana, and promoted by the Department of Social Welfare and the Biennale Foundation of Valencia, is on show as part of 'The Ideal City', the 2003 Valencia Biennale.

With 17 innovative architects each designing parts of the scheme, including Toyo Ito, Foreign Office Architects, Abalos & Herreros, Actar, MVRDV, François Roche, Duncan Lewis and Guallart himself, SocióPolis aims to develop a residential complex – a social campus, no less – for different vulnerable social groups (for example, old people, young people and single parents). Set on the border of Valencia, it is based on the construction of 'a habitat of solidarity'[4] in which social interaction is facilitated. Here, the latest technologies within domestic space are applied in an overall hybridisation of the urban with rural nature, architecture and landscape, including such urban-rural resources (of which the allotment is one example) as a market garden.

The master plan is to be developed on the lines of the *hortulus*, or medieval garden residence, in which the house is set within a natural, productive environment. Each building comes with its own plot of land, to which a specific market-garden crop and density is assigned, and the infrastructure includes a running track.

Each building will have a hybrid programme with residential units and public systems side by side, and the locations and typologies have been adopted in order to maximise social interaction. The housing is rental accommodation, aimed at users excluded from social provision, and includes a home for the elderly, a social information centre and a day centre for autistic children, and is built within the economic constraints of social housing. Guallart's argument is that typological innovation is necessary because traditional social housing in Spain has been designed for typical family models that have now evolved into diversified patterns. SocióPolis is a 'slow city' with a high environmental quality that runs in parallel to the hyper development of the global world. ◬

Notes
1. See www.africaserver.nl/hg/introduction
2. Franz Sumnitsch, interview with the author, 12 February 2003.
3. Alex de Rijke of dRMM, interview with the author, 15 September 2002.
4. Vicente Guallart, interview with the author, 12 April 2003.

'The Ideal City' runs until 6 September 2003 (www.masdearte.com/bienaldevalencia)

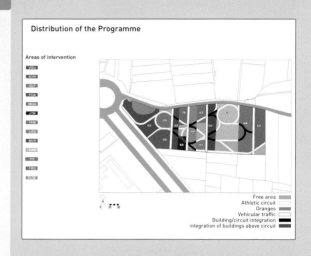

Distribution of the Programme

Areas of intervention

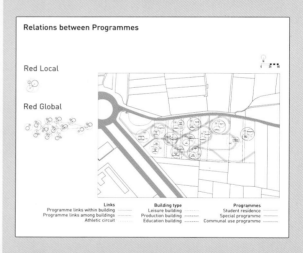

Relations between Programmes

Red Local

Red Global

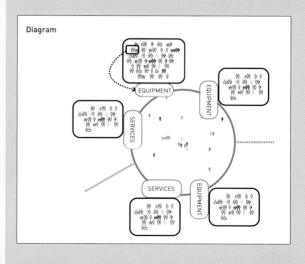

Diagram

Working the Programme:
Designing Social and Affordable Housing in the Netherlands

Across the world, the Netherlands is commonly held up as a model of European social responsibility. **Lucy Bullivant** lifts the lid on the state of Dutch housing, which since the late 1980s has been left to the vicissitudes of the market. She explains how the introduction of a greater uniformity by developers has often left architects frustrated and the public yearning for difference. Against this backdrop she shows some inspired projects that seek to play with and hybridise housing models.

When you visit the Netherlands, you carry a sense of being in an urbanised country, where architecture benefits from integrated government policies devised well in advance that embrace not just that discipline but landscape design and urban planning. The view of the landscape when flying in a Tulip Air jet from Rotterdam to Amsterdam is also a dramatic reminder of how ordered and yet imaginative is the use of land in all its contrasting forms, the result of close attention to what is, after all, an intrinsically artificial landscape. Longitudinally divided streets give everyone, especially cyclists – small family units in transit, and also individuals quite often hurtling along their 'track' without their lights on – their space. But you had better not cross these well-defined borders without carefully scrutinising the tracks, preferably with eyes in the back of your head.

Environmental space in the Netherlands, being at a premium, is thought of in its totality, and any tendency to urban sprawl is a matter to be culturally monitored; exhibitions of new proposals advancing the role of design

in differentiating lifestyle abound, and everything, superficially, seems in a state of bright-eyed optimism about the creative power it exerts in society.

But how are architectural design and urban planning responding to the housing needs of an increasingly culturally diversified, network society, one in which the market has rolled forward and state provision has retreated? In what ways can architects have an impact on the provision of social and affordable housing within the existing setup of disjunction and transition, and how can design render 'difference' nonetheless translatable into the Dutch adherence to equality in so many aspects of life, and vice versa?

Dutch government policies favour a condition of working behind urban planning and its bureaucracy – 'behind the curtain' – in response to what Joost Schrijnen, former Rotterdam city planner at the dS+V (dienst Stedebouw+Volkshuisvesting) describes as the necessity to find out what the potentials of planning are.[1] The Netherlands Architecture Institute in Rotterdam, opened in 1993, has played an active promotional role here. It recently invited the public to debate the whole social fabric of the Netherlands, with the result that parliament elected not to build certain schemes. In 2002, the Amsterdam architectural

Above
West 8 urban design and landscape architecture, Borneo Sporenburg, Amsterdam (realised 1996–2000), a widely acclaimed urban design in the city's former dockland area, Oostelijk Havengebied.

NL Architects, Roof Road NT, Amsterdam, 2001

This project consists of 210 single-family dwellings in four
categories/types and 80 apartments in the VINEX area, close
to the Hague. Here, NL Architects has put the terrace house,
a widely appreciated traditional Dutch typology, up for
reconsideration. Over 80 per cent of people in the Netherlands,
the architects claim, desire to live in a suburb, in a house with
a garden, with cars in front of the door, and where kids can play
safely. But they point to a remarkable ambiguity in the way the
Dutch are dealing with suburbanisation, namely the strategies
laid down by VINEX, which state that all new housing should
emerge in direct proximity to existing centres; the consumer
should be taken into account, and the market should dictate
the production. Compact cities, efficient infrastructure and
a relatively intact landscape should be the outcome. In the
1990s, when the policy was conceived, automobility was a
phenomenon to be repressed, and as a consequence the
position of the car in VINEX was never resolved, says NL.

As the VINEX densities are too high to fulfil people's wishes,
suburbs without gardens are starting to be developed. Roads
and parking take up 37 per cent of the surface, while more
than 55 per cent of the materials used is solid (tarmac,
concrete or bricks). However, densities are still too low to
call the condition urban.

NL's Roof Road NT aims to create a car-free zone that at
the same time is fully accessible. Their trick is putting the
access roads and parking on the roofs of terrace housing.
By combining infrastructure and building, and by turning
roof into road, an additional 25 per cent of the total surface
is gained, a quarter extra space by comparison with VINEX.
This surplus is then available for public or semipublic use,
for playgrounds and more extensive individual gardens.

The other asset NL identifies as emerging from its
reinvention of the terrace house is the chance to escape the
compactness that usually comes with what the architects see
as the typical layout of the VINEX developments, instead, opening
up the mostly claustrophobic environment. And by positioning
the driveway on top of the houses, the roof offers a panoramic
view while the ground level is car-free and child-friendly.

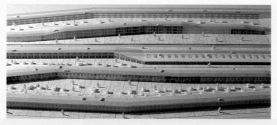

organisation ARCAM's map of the Netherlands,[2] displayed at 50 x 50 kilometre scale, summarised all spatial development plans and programmes on which work would start by 2010, revealing a lack of cooperation by the municipalities and a fragmentation of the areas intended for expansion. This second exercise in transparency originated from the perception that planners know what they will do in the next 10 years, but the public does not. It was offered as a catalyst for communication about planning that transgressed municipal borders.

During the heavy bombing and destruction of the Second World War, all building activity was stopped, and by 1945 there was a total housing shortage of over 300,000 dwellings. Subsequent reconstruction was based on a planned approach, giving the government a central role in relation to production, distribution and consumption. Standardised housing systems were put in place, eventually leading to a complete industrialisation of building in bigger units – volume as well as surface.

The ideal was of *wijgedacht* (a socially well-balanced community), with architecture the 'three dimensional expression of human relationships', as architect Jacob Bakema defined it. Together with JH van den Broek, Bakema designed the Lijnbaan shopping centre in the centre of Rotterdam, a unique and widely copied pedestrianised shopping area resembling an open-air mall. Apartments here are not located above retail establishments, as in traditional shopping areas, but in separate buildings behind the Lijnbaan. Compact compositions meeting the needs of all were the answer.

In the 1970s new housing-types[4] developed a closer relationship to their surroundings, and during the following decade obsolete industrial areas within cities were transformed into high-density housing and administrative centres. After a long period of involvement by the state, housing was finally left largely to the market. In the wake of this drastic step by the government, subsidies were withdrawn in 1995, obliging housing associations to change their roles and become development agencies. This government retreat from housing construction, as architectural critic Hans Ibelings has pointed out, had led to a swift decline in the volume of subsidised housing in relation to the Netherlands' total housing production.[5] The government's Fourth Spatial Planning Report (1988)[6] had 10 years earlier created a framework for a substantial production of

dwellings at low density envisaged until 2005, spreading (or even sprawling) into the limited open space available. A supplement to this published in 1993, entitled the 'Vierde Nota Ruimtelijke Ordening Extra' (Fourth Extra Spatial Policy) – the VINEX Planning Report – laid down a housing programme of 800,000 dwellings to be built in neighbourhoods close to existing cities, between 1995 and 2005. This required new tactics. Not only did the associations change their role, but, as architectural critic Hans van Dijk spelled it out last year, 'increasingly architects are expected to respond to market demands rather than be concerned with good intentions'.[7]

Was this the unfurling of a form of social tragicomedy? After all, provision for social housing is enshrined within Dutch culture. Its first legal framework was laid down in the Housing Act of 1901, and earlier in the 19th century plenty of architectural experimentation took place whereby building form was not dictated by programme. As Aaron Betsky, director of the Netherlands Architecture Institute recently explained, the institutors of the 1901 Act had 'worked out a way of creating shelter and subsidising the differential between renting and purchase for those that could not afford housing – and, from this, in aggregate, a city'.[8] This 20th-century social remit for the country covered housing financed by non-profit housing associations as well as the state, and required local councils overseeing communities with over 10,000 inhabitants to create development schemes. It provided 'an architecture of grand purpose and mass need'[9] that was neither explicitly suburban in its use of land nor about creating repetitive blocks. 'It was about using form to create generous public spaces'.[10] Betsky adds that it is that whole ethos which is now 'threatened by public developers telling people these spaces should be privatised'.[11]

The Dutch government maintained this commitment, responding decisively over the decades of the 20th century, particularly after the Second World War when it was faced with recurrent housing shortages. Recently, however, the country has been experiencing a situation where only 36 per cent of the total housing stock consists of social housing, available to rent and invariably of good quality,[12] whereas in earlier decades this figure was much higher. Outside the Netherlands, with the exception of a few Western European countries, social housing is specifically intended for households with limited societal options. By contrast, the Dutch social-housing sector accommodates a differentiated group. Consequently, tenants bear no stigma.

Ideas for urban development and housing have long since been strongly interrelated, with public housing not a marginal issue but one strongly related to wider social issues, and architects have always played an important

West 8 urban design & landscape architecture
Borneo Sporenburg, Amsterdam (realised 1996–2000)

West 8's interpretation of 'high density' means master plans with a 'low-rise, architectonic diversity'. The practice's Borneo Sporenburg master plan for two peninsulas in the eastern part of Amsterdam's former large-scale dockland area of Oostelijk Havengebied responded to the city council's request for mainly low-rise housing for families with children, providing 2,500 dwelling units in low rise – that is, a density of 100 units per hectare – grouped around the two docks, Borneo and Sporenburg.

These points of departure offered a unique opportunity for an urban experiment. West 8, which guided a team of five developers, produced an innovative typology of three-storey ground-accessed houses that depart from the usual terraced or traditional Dutch canal house by the inclusion of facilities usually standard in the private realm, for example individual patios and roof gardens.

Much of what would normally be designed as public space is included in the plots to be developed, thereby creating space within the walls of the buildings. By repeating this type in a great variety of dwelling modes, from social housing to exclusive apartments, and with a maximum architectural variation, West 8 gives birth to a lively and variegated street elevation. A balance is achieved between the repetition of the individual dwellings, the roofscape and the hulking scale of the docks themselves. The interaction of high and low rise creates an urban fabric, orientation and structure.

role in the process.[13] The Netherlands' history of affordable housing, and its role in economic life, have in the past created social stability. Low rent helped keep a cap on wage packets, thus supporting industry; avoidance of overproduction of new housing maintained an appropriate scale of housing resource, in case of higher unemployment later on. This set of interrelations was overseen by a well-organised system with many active players. Housing corporations, governmental subsidy policies, good urban plans, the involvement of high-quality architects in social housing, a wide variety of prototypes and a balance between public and private interests, combined to create a marked effect.

> Low rent helped keep a cap on wage packets, thus supporting industry; avoidance of overproduction of new housing maintained an appropriate scale of housing resource, in case of higher unemployment later on.

However, there is now a perception among architects in the Netherlands that although social housing is certainly not dying out as a type of commission, it is subject to new frustrations. Its occupation of one-third of a project still needs to be sponsored by the other housing categories, but factors such as the attitude of the client and the housing association also play a role here. Architect Kees Christiaanse, for example, explained a few years ago that in designing his Koekoeksweg housing at Amersfoort (1995–7) he managed to overcome the client's limited scope for use of the floor area. He did this through the design of a projecting gallery structure in timber serving as a common meeting area and threshold between private and public zones. This was an exception, he asserted, as most associations were determined to stick with a concrete structure.[14]

Deregulation and privatisation have not necessarily led to risk taking. Not only have the housing associations been privatised, but there has been a wider shift from rented to owner-occupied housing sold by commercial developers. The gap between social housing and housing to buy has narrowed, with the latter, available on the market and also getting more expensive, part of a bigger European pattern.

Amidst this trend, the Dutch government has at the same time been encouraging house purchase, something Hans Ibelings denounces as the translation of a basic human right into 'a Thatcherite doctrine'.[15]

Times have indeed changed. When it comes to the opportunities for architects to build social housing five or six years ago, one could talk about wider horizons with scope to realise different typologies. Now on the front line in negotiations about future jobs, architects who are social housing specialists see developers preferring to redevelop plans already made for the inner city. In the Netherlands it is policy to finish an urban plan, otherwise the result is leftover plots of ground for house building that lose a certain coherence. The problem can then arise, as Rotterdam-based architect Gerard Macreanor has explained, that the old plan does not offer a relationship between the realms of public and private.[16] The question of physical clarity between public, semipublic/private and private space in line with changing patterns of behaviour almost inevitably begs to be scrutinised.

The Netherlands has always been characterised by rationalised building practices that can be manipulated within certain limits. And the financial limitations to which Rem Koolhaas bluntly responded 'no money, no details', impose themselves even more forcefully with regard to the economic stringencies of social-housing budgets. The current mood among developers in Amsterdam when it comes to new social housing is now tending towards 'keep it simple'. After the profusion of typologies of the last five or six years has come a move to reductive solutions, but in the end this is counterproductive, in that the dwellings that result look so alike that people hesitate to buy them.

The need to meet acute housing needs in and on the outskirts of urban areas and buck the trend for a cultural tradition of standardisation in housing design has nonetheless in recent years paved the way for a continuous flow of new low-cost solutions and for deregulated 'wild house building'. This concept became famous in the Dutch media in 1997, and among the throng talking about the necessary power the consumer had to exercise in housing matters was the architect Carel Weeber who asked: Why is everything so regulated? Why can't people live in holiday homes, like campers? Is there no room for individual expression? Why is it not possible to put your own house on your own piece of land?[17] Weeber remonstrated that citizens could buy a piece of polder, but not their own ground.

Prototypical housing design schemes extending traditional forms are now common. They fulfil both Weeber's romantic vision of untrammelled, deregulated developments and the privatised schemes of developers produced in the wake of the retreat of the government. The fact that different ministries have been responsible

Notes
1. Joost Schrijnen, lecture at the Architecture Foundation's Architecture Centres Conference, British Museum, London, 13 June 2002.
2. ARCAM, Amsterdam's Centre for Architecture, www.arcam.nl.
3. Hans van Dijk, 1990–2000: Architecture in the Netherlands, a Chronology, Faculty of Architecture, Technical University of Delft, 2002.
4. Advocates of housing with a greater flexibility in use in this era include John Habraken, in Jonathan Teicher (ed) Supports: An Alternative to Mass Housing, Urban Press (London), English edition,1972. A reprint of the 1972 edition was published in 1999; see www.habraken.com.
5. In the mid-1980s, subsidised housing accounted for about 90 per cent of all new housing; by 1996 that percentage had dropped to just 30 per cent. Hans Ibelings, 'Variation in housing in the 1990s', in Arjen Oosterman, Housing in the Netherlands: Exemplary Architecture of the Nineties, NAi (Rotterdam), 1998, p 13.
6. The Fourth Spatial Planning Report, or 'Vierde Nota

Architectenbureau Marlies Rohmer
Borneo-Eiland Housing, Amsterdam (realised 2001)

As part of his overall master plan for the Borneo Sporenburg former docklands area, Adriaan Geuze of West 8 wanted a form of low-rise high-density housing in big blocks. Most are 40 metres deep. Layered views, like inner courts, are common, with family houses on the outside over three layers with a harbour-like exterior. Marlies Rohmer was one of a number of architects commissioned to design housing schemes on the Borneo peninsular within the West 8 master plan. (66 houses and 21 atelier units with a budget of 4.5 million euros). She addresses the reality that public space does not belong to anybody now that state authorities in the Netherlands have withdrawn their role, giving it to the market. As a result, no one is responsible for the squares, parks and public gardens and the result is total neglect.

The Borneo-Eiland houses have a multifunctional ground floor and a transitional zone, and on the street side the houses have large kitchens that function as living rooms or home offices. Placing such a multifunctional space on the ground floor livens up the street. With their half-open farmhouse doors, occupants can get 'a verandah feeling' of partly sitting outside in the street, in a communal eating place. This porch provides an almost unnoticeable transition from private to public space. Rohmer argues that private space has changed very little over the centuries – everybody behaves as they please in the privacy of their own house, whether a luxury villa or cheap rented apartment.

Rohmer addresses the reality that parents will no longer allow their children to play in the streets alone, and are often too tied up to walk them to the playground, by creating a wide pavement area in front of the houses which is maintained by the residents themselves, providing a space where children can play under supervision.

Ruimtelijke Ordening' (1988), and the Extra papers published in the early 1990s, were part of a series of Dutch Government papers on environmental planning policy. The Fifth Report in the series was published in 2000.

7. Van Dijk, op cit.

8. This provided the associations with up to 8 per cent of the total construction budget.

9. Aaron Betsky, lecture, Architecture Association, London, 28 January 2003.

10. Ibid.

11. Ibid.

12. André Ouwehand and Gelske van Daalen, *Dutch Housing Associations: A Model for Social Housing*, Delft University Press, 2002.

13. Noud de Vreeze, lecture at Burghers in Suburbia, Holland 1998–2010, conference staged in 1998 at the Architectural Association, London, curated by Irénée Scalbert.

14. Kees Christiaanse, in Kathy Battista and Florian Migsch, *The Netherlands: A Guide to Recent Architecture*, Ellipsis (London), 1998, pp 180–1.

15. Hans Ibelings, op cit, p 22.

16. Interview with the author, 11 April 2003.

17. For a discussion about planning policies and privatisation, see the interview with Dutch Labour Party MP Adri Duivesteijn by Ole Bouman, 'I'm putting the whole social housing system on the line', *Archis*, 6, 1997, pp 22–3.

18. Ole Bouman, 'Inaction as accomplishment', editorial in *Archis*, 10, 1999, pp 4–5, special issue on 'The Rise of the Housing Consumer'.

19. Kamiel Klasse, NL Architects, interview with the author, 10 December 2002.

20. Almere, a new town near the north of the Randstad and the Gooi region of the Netherlands, was built on a polder in 1968, and has been described by Ole Bouman as having 'a place where we can study what happens when an urban extension scheme reaches the critical mass at which it itself becomes a city', arguably not possible in the VINEX developments. Ole Bouman, editorial in 'Almere, Leisure City' issue of *Archis*, 11, 1999.

21. Quoted by Arthur Wortmann in 'An architecture governed by viewing figures: building houses on uncontrolled plots', *Archis*, 10, 1999.

22. A phrase coined by Bernard Hulsman, in Bernard Hulsman, Hans van Rossum, Frank van Wijk and Lodewijk Baljon, 'Give VINEX more space', in *Een stad in uitersten*, NAi (Rotterdam), 2001. See also Ed Melet's essay in 'Olanda', special issue of *Abitare*, 417, May 2002, pp 198–201 and 294–5.

23. Adriaan Geuze, *Colonizing the Void*, NAi (Rotterdam), 1996, exhibition catalogue published to accompany the exhibition curated by architect Geuze, director of West 8, at the Dutch pavilion at the Venice Architecture Biennale 1996.

24. Interview with the author, 13 June 2002.

for promoting each of these housing solutions does not mean quality across the board should not be encouraged, as *Archis* editor-in chief Ole Bouman has said.[18] The wealth of new ideas emerging in the last few years also shows that variety can be achieved despite the mix of old and newly accentuated limitations, and responses can be made to uniformity. On a critical level this is an application of pure spatial design to find optimum solutions.

An ingredient of the present-day culture is the car, representing an individual's personal achievement of mobility, which needs to be designed for as an integrated part of a whole housing design, without dominating it. But equally large issues are that, first, the boundaries between public and private space are now much more easily blurred, and, second, that innovative design is badly needed to cater for maximum social diversity. Providing the terms of the mandate to extend housing provision, VINEX promoted compact cities, but in their proposal for the Roof Road (see earlier) NL Architects argue against its stipulations. A reinvention of the typical terrace house for a culture of mobility, the design epitomises the fact that the densities in VINEX are too high to successfully reward all consumer wishes, while also being too low to consider the condition urban.[19]

Opinions are divided regarding the impact of VINEX schemes that 'hook' on to existing infrastructure. Apart from the Ijburg near the centre of Amsterdam (18,000 new homes), the largest are at Leidsche Rijn near Utrecht (plans for 30,000 homes) and Ypenburg near the Hague (12,000 homes). It is worth setting these developments alongside that of the city of Almere (plans to expand from 160,000 to 250,000 by 2010).[20] Some feel that while this government-initiated project embodies a 'we know what people like' mentality, it in fact lacks flexibility in social models, with all-too-small houses and gardens – a mono-solution out of step with social changes. In 2000, a third of the housing in the VINEX locations was made available as uncontrolled plots to private clients. Some critics[21] feel the first ones are guilty of this, but defend VINEX locations built more recently on grounds of scale and facilities and as sites of continual experiment. Will the earlier ones need to be revised in a few years, as is speculated?

In their housing projects, architects like NL in Amsterdam openly challenge the compactness of the densities of the VINEX locations, their reliance on the market, and moreover their failure to address the phenomenon of

automobility. As a project, VINEX began when the government announced that it no longer wished to be responsible for urban planning, and would instead sell bits of ground. Dubbed 'network cities',[22] VINEX projects have also been defended on the grounds that they do not need to provide urban layered space, and represent the evolution of regional urbanity. The value of the projects may be that they counter a new urban intensity that goes beyond technically measurable density. This is something that has spawned a renewed interest in the 'vertical city' (Mecanoo's Montevideo, now on site in Rotterdam's Kop van Zuid, and Rem Koolhaas's de Rotterdam to be built nearby, awaiting the go-ahead), with something more apparently traditional.

However, it is not in the allocated downtown VINEX areas but in an extension of the city of Amsterdam that the highest density, and a wider diversity of housing, have been achieved, including social housing. In the Borneo-Sporenburg master plan (see earlier) by Adriaan Geuze/West 8 at Amsterdam's eastern docklands, not only does Geuze avoid the traditional typology of the narrow terrace house, but he makes the social housing present within the scheme a landmark for the area, visible from a distance.

It was of course Adriaan Geuze who most dramatically presented a galling vision of a million identical houses at the 1999 Venice Biennale in the form of an enormous swathe of identical tiny plain wooden blocks shaped like a house with a typical pitch roof laid out on the floor to compose a map of the Netherlands.[23] His 'In Holland staat een huis' exhibition, displayed to an international audience, was a response to the officially declared need of the VINEX policies for over a million new dwellings in the Netherlands. The standard terraced house as an answer to affordable housing had already filled the Netherlands for decades.

The Dutch Ministry of Housing, Spatial Planning and the Environment (VROM) was set up to make sense of the physical arrangement of the Netherlands, and latterly, what Betsky calls 'the compaction of market forces that act on the Dutch landscape'.[24] While there has been a long history of integrated solutions, and the weaving in of infill areas due to the compressed nature of space, market-led practices have now brought about another trend. This is the combining of mixed programmes in housing, both desirable socially and functional in terms of a compact use of the landscape. Kees Christiaanse's 1999 scheme at Leidschenveen, Utrecht, reflects this, compacting or combining social housing with highly marketable lofts along irrigation ditches, fitting into the proportions of the man-made landscape.

Amsterdam-based architect Marlies Rohmer observes in recent Dutch architecture a diversification of forms of collectivity after a period of individuality.[25] For example, as a result of the increasing average age of the population and the more dynamic elderly,

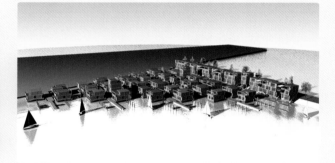

but also because of events such as 11 September, new collective forms of living together are developing. While suggesting safety and social contact, Rohmer maintains that if negatively formulated these concepts might also induce segregation and ghettoisation (tending towards gated communities). She refers to a film she was stimulated by, *Una Giornata Particulare*, in which there is a central space in the housing community where people can easily meet yet effortlessly find their privacy if they want to, fulfilling both individual and collective needs. For Rohmer, the concept of sustainability is not simple to grasp, and at the same time it is hard to manipulate social change. Her work, evolved from research into changes within the family, is one answer to the looming 'expiration date' to which housing is increasingly subjected in the wake of social changes in the way communication takes place.

One factor among many that may assist the realisation of social housing that is both feasible within strict financial limits yet nonetheless an embodiment of a more flexible type, is how extensively it can be determined by its occupants. The idea that a building can be personally customised is popular, as epitomised in Kas

Oosterhuis and Ilona Lenard of Oosterhuis.nl's prefabricated Variomatic houses[26] being built in Zoetermeer outside the Hague, which set production, promotion and consumption into the frame of consumer choice.

Social housing is clearly related to the social and economic revitalisation of urbanised developments, a perception specialists in the UK are now linking more closely to the wider European use of brownfield sites,[27] and of which local government in some cities is increasingly aware. In Paris, the socialist mayor Bertrand Delanoe some time ago went as far as to start buying up luxury properties in chic *arrondissements* in the west and centre of the city for conversion into low-rent accommodation for the working class (named HLMs, or *Habitations a Loyer Moderé*). One of the many contradictions thrown up by the Dutch social housing system being both far more widely and traditionally provided and mostly allocated through need, not financial eligibility, is that it needs to evolve in step, qualitatively, with the Dutch market-led housing phenomenon. This in turn is responding in its own right to evolving patterns of differentiation in social behaviour.

Although mixed-use housing developments are nothing new in the Netherlands, they do not preclude the continuation of rigid parameters of provision. Another factor is that complexes mixing subsidised, unsubsidised and purchased dwellings also betray the

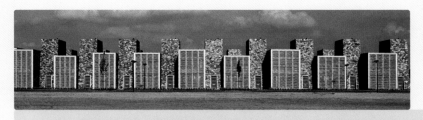

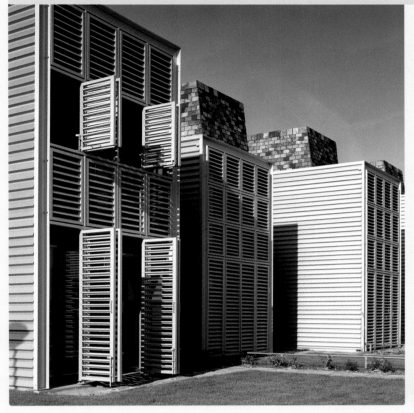

For the outdoor Expo at Almere, Marlies Rohmer designed an experimental scheme of 18 houses working to a total budget of 2,040,000 euros based on an emerging demographic: the increasing average age of the population, and the number, and dynamic and mobile lifestyles of senior citizens (dubbed 'snowbirds' in the us, these are elderly people without a home or permanent place to live who travel with a camper or mobile home fitted out with amenities).

The conceptual image (below) shows three-storey housing blocks, flanked by trailers, providing the inspiration for an accompanying space that is modular. Of variable length, width and height, a metal-clad module, also called a 'canopy', has a standardised core and includes a kitchen, double-height living area and two bedrooms on the first floor; the block, with its reconstituted-stone cladding, houses the services and the stairs. Rohmer calls this a 'stove house', as it is the shape of a stove, diminishing in size towards the roof, on which is a roof terrace.

Rohmer envisages the modular element clad in metal panels, which have a hermetic appearance when shut, and open out on the garden side.

25. Marlies Rohmer, 'Expiration date', lecture, Barcelona, March 2003.
26 See www.osterhuis.nl and www.archcenter.ru/eng/council/oosterhuis.
27. See also Mark Stephens, Nicky Burns and Lisa MacKay, *Social Market or Safety Net: British Social Rented Housing in a European Context, a Comprehensive Overview of the Links Between Social Policies and Housing Policies in Europe, Specifically in the uk, the Netherlands, Denmark, Sweden and France*, Policy Press (Glasgow), 2002. An initiative supported by the Joseph Rowntree Foundation.
28. See *Archis*, 3, 1999, special issue on Bijlmermeer.
29. Chairman of the Architectural Association, chairing at Burghers in Suburbia conference, Architectural Association, London, 1998.
30. Aaron Betsky lecture, Architectural Association, Burghers in Suburbia conference, Architectural Association, London, 1998.
31. Interview with Marco Vermeulen, 6 January 2003. See Berci Florian, Hans Mommas, Michael Speaks, Koen van Synghel and Marco Vermeulen, *City Branding: Image Building and Building Images*, compiled and edited by Urban Affairs (Theo Hauben and Marco Vermeulen) and Véronique Patteeuw, NAi (Rotterdam), 2002.

notion of equality. They do this through siting; for example, social-housing occupants get the communal spaces, purchasers get the most internal space and the best views of the surrounding landscape from their position on the edge of the site (though this specific example may not necessarily be a disadvantageous arrangement to the former) and treatment of the facade, inevitably privileged over the floor plan. As Mohsen Mostafavi has asked: How do you reconcile the role of the individual in the collective if this is not carried out at the level of architectural representation?[29] When architects want to experiment with the rules specifically governing social housing design, as they frequently do, it sounds like a tall order. Fortunately it is clear that architects from both large practices such as Kees Christiaanse's kcap and smaller teams at Urban Affairs, also Rotterdam-based, are giving a lot of attention to the interconnection and, where possible, the hybridisation of typologies. In realising social housing, as Francine Houben, co-founder of Mecanoo has stated, the rules are easier to stretch if the architect is also the urban planner of a site.

Aaron Betsky terms this overall process as manipulating form within tradition. In a society

where, as he says, 'nothing escapes ... everything folds into itself',[30] when it comes to maintaining yet evolving the innately Dutch concept of the 'polder model where everyone is happy', the challenge is surely to create space for difference. This is not only a First World housing marketing concept now fed with children's milk, but also a cultural hybridisation of form and landscape, inside and outside, public and private.
Hardly a new global phenomenon, yet in a phase of fast evolution it is partly a result of the new technologies revolutionising our concept of space as well as time.

Hybridisation is a response to density and itself a densification – or intensification – of space, as well as a continual challenge to 'restate nature' (as Betsky puts it). Include human nature in that definition, and the challenge of 'hybrid' design applied to social and affordable housing remains one of rendering it a cultural process that is manipulable in its own right. Traditional notions of the collective may be in danger of being eradicated. However, if the limits of that manipulability of design, technical and programmatic factors are recognised, social principles that are in themselves desirably adaptable as patterns of use evolve, yet not so much so that the market gets to call too many of the shots, can then be held on to. ∆

Marlies Rohmer, as the urban planners of the project, are designing a predominantly social-housing scheme in the Bijmermeer, a high-rise housing complex realised in Amsterdam in 1968,[28] creating a new version of the gated community. Instead of knocking it down and putting low rise in its place, the estate is given twisted towers on the street (designed by NL Architects), its beautiful garages are retained and new islands are proposed with simple new flats and glazing reminiscent of Jean Nouvel's Cartier Fondation in Paris. There was a big problem of undefined greenery, so the architecture now makes a link to the green area, giving the 'transformed towers an an organic attitude', as Rohmer describes it.

The diagram below indicates specific interventions to improve the quality of living.

The extremely low construction budget of 3.1 million euros for this project led to the design of 44 minimal 100-square-metre base dwellings with maximal expansion possibilities including through a glass conservatory or a roof extension. Both options are as wide as the dwelling itself and expand the cubic capacity to 150 square metres.

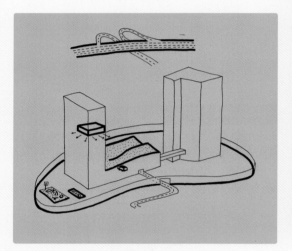

At Nieuw Terbregge, one of Rotterdam's inner-city VINEX extension areas on the Rotte river, Mecanoo, on this project given the role of both architect and urban planner, was in a position to create an alternative to the all-too-prevalent standard terrace house.

There are two strategies. First, 48 'waterfront houses' in an 'eight-under-one-roof typology' sit by the side of the canal, a concept the architects developed several years ago in Arnhem with the same contractor. The houses form groups of eight, looking from a distance like grand mansions. Each has its own garden or deck above the water, and the typological composition is well thought through with the four middle-placed houses cheaper than those on the perimeter. In Arnhem the blocks were placed in an orchard; those in Rotterdam have been placed so that they extend over the water.

Creating good connections between domestic and public space characterises the other main high-density scheme on the site, in *de Landjes* (little lands), 'dwellings divided in four peninsulas grouped around living decks'. The car-parking areas are covered with a wooden deck creating outdoor space between the housing blocks. This can be used as a playground, a terrace or communal space (with a power plant at the ends), freeing up this pedestrian area from cars and their garages and creating 'double-decker' accommodation. Between the two, a multitude of holes connects the two levels spatially and allows trees to grow through them while the lower level stays light. The rhythm of the disorderly placed blocks creates a unity on each peninsula, and the backyard of the dwellings is placed directly next to the water. On their ends, and on the waterfront facades, an orange-brown brickwork is combined with white varnished wood. Here little windows jump for attention, accentuating further the impression of a variegated environment of height differences, gardens, piers over the water, which eventually will be covered with more of a 'scarf' of greenery.

The 107 double-deckers and the 48 waterfront dwellings underline the need to create new typologies, a quest the practice says can only succeed when the design team is both architect and urban planner. Typological innovation and diversity fulfils changing social needs in a way that is not only balanced but blurs the boundaries between public and private areas, enriching the space in and around housing for the residents' own imaginative social programmes. At the same time, new dwellings, whether in the Netherlands where space is at a premium or in cities elsewhere, should be capable of withstanding social and spatial change in the future.

Above and below: **Dwelling 1**　　Below: **Dwelling 2**　　Above and below: **Dwelling 3**

Urban Affairs and Joep Mol Architects I never promised you a rose garden, Godschalk Rosemondtstraat, Eindhoven (realised 2002)

In a setting that is a cross between a garden and a building, three single-person dwellings were created in the outbuildings of a former steam laundry with upstairs accommodation dating from 1934. The project is an example of how comfortable high-density dwellings can be accommodated in former work spaces on plots located behind the typical ribbon development in Eindhoven, promoting the identity of the neighbourhood and contributing to the renewal of the industrial town – once flourishing and more recently usurped as a place to live by Amsterdam – and creating domestic settings with a 'negotiable' meaning. By making an effort to develop existing qualities of a city like Eindhoven into a sustainable image, says Marco Vermeulen of Urban Affairs, the present 'building images' would then evolve into 'image building'.[31]

The dwellings are organised in three zones found in the original spatial configuration. Two of them make optimal use of the existing building structure and spatial qualities; the third is situated in a new volume on the street side of the plot and adds a striking element to the streetscape.

Dwelling 1 is situated at the rear of the development. Here, the interior space is encroached upon in two places:

first, the car can drive right into the living room in brutal fashion, its headlights announcing the driver's arrival. Midway along the hall a small swimming pool pushes into the roofing felt; you can also shower on the roof.

Dwelling 2 is a new three-level volume on the street side of the site, with two parking spaces accessed directly from the street. The living level extends over the cars, its interior showcased behind the glazed front with an enormous cruciform glazing bar. Bathroom, storage and hall are located on ground level. The bedroom is romantically located on an aluminium summer house on the roof terrace, from which the raised living room offers a view of the street below.

Dwelling 3 is between Dwelling 1 and the block of existing dwellings on the street. Raising a few beams and lowering a few creates spaces for a raised bed and an elegant roof profile allowing more light to penetrate. A hothouse for roses shelters the 5-metre-high blue tiled cubicle on the roof. A stair of steel rises from the communal bicycle shed next to the dwelling to the roof terrace of the adjoining apartment complex.

The use of bitumen felt on the roofs and facades of the three dwellings gives continuity to the whole project, and the swap in functions – hothouse for roses as bathroom, *bankirai* garden fence as safety net – harmonises with the existing elements in the surrounding gardens.

The Regenerator
Profile of Tom Bloxham of Urban Splash

Right
Tom Bloxham of Urban Splash.

Above, left to right
Before and after development.

Concert Square, Liverpool,
in 1993 and 1995. (Designed
by Ian Simpson Architects.)

Smithfield Buildings,
Manchester, in 1995 and 1998.
(Designed by Stephenson Bell.)

Britannia Mills, Britannia
Basin, Manchester, in 1998
and 2000. (Designed by
in-house architects.)

In the last 10 years, Urban Splash has become synonymous with high-quality design and city-centre living in Manchester and Liverpool. **Helen Castle** profiles its chair, Tom Bloxham, and tracks his rise from market-stall holder to a major developer in the Northwest. As the company takes a new direction investing in a major regeneration project at Ancoats with Alsop Architects in east Manchester and a luxury development with Foster and Partners at Altrincham, just outside the city, what might the future hold for these new-scale outer-urban ventures?

Above, left to right
Before and after development.

Old Haymarket, Liverpool, in
1998 and 2000. (Designed by
Urban Splash in-house
architects, now Arkheion
Architects.)

Box Works, Britannia Basin,
Manchester, in 2000 and 2001.
(Designed by Arkheion
Architects.)

Timber Wharf, Britannia Basin,
Manchester, in 2000 and 2002.
(Designed by Glenn Howells
Architects).

As group chairman and co-founder of
Manchester-based property development
company Urban Splash, Tom Bloxham has
played a key role in the regeneration of the
Northwest. Although Urban Splash has been in
business for only a decade, Bloxham has already
been acknowledged by the Establishment for
his efforts. In 1999 he received an MBE in the
Queen's Honours for Services to Architecture
and Regeneration. He was also invited to serve
on the Urban Sounding Board as a personal
source of advice to Lord Falconer, and to become
chair of the North West Arts Board. In 2002 RIBA
voted Urban Splash as Client of the Year 'for
their commitment to both design quality and
regeneration'. And every single scheme the
firm has built has gained a RIBA design award.

It is as if Bloxham and his colleagues have
acquired a Midas touch when it comes to property
development and its design. When I am being
shown around Timber Wharf by Urban Splash's
PR, she tells me that as soon as Bloxham's car,
with its distinctive personalised number plates,
is spotted in the vicinity in Manchester, the
property prices immediately shoot up. This may
be a good bit of publicity but Bloxham has gained
the status of something of a local folk hero – a
south London barrow boy made good.

Despite his university education, his previous career
selling fire extinguishers off the back of a van is flagged
up on Urban Splash's website. What rings true about
this image of Bloxham is that he has a rare ability to
communicate with a raw enthusiasm, which is further
underlaid by commercial nous and a certain toughness.
This all adds up to him being an engaging front man
and spokesperson. The promotional video made last
year for New Islington, the major regeneration scheme
that Urban Splash is undertaking in east Manchester,
features a windswept Bloxham eulogising on site.
Alone he walks purposefully along the banks of the
Ashton Canal – currently a scene of complete dereliction
and decay with boarded-up houses surrounded by
scrubland – enthusing about his vision for a 'New
Manchesterdam'. It is a performance that, according to
Building Design, has turned the video into a cult item.[1]

To date, Urban Splash has largely made its name
through loft developments and small-scale commercial
spaces, either as warehouse conversions or new builds
adjacent to converted buildings. At Castlefield in
Manchester, the firm renovated and converted the
19th-century warehouses, Britannia Mills (2000), and an
Art Deco building, Box Works (2001), with its in-house
architects, who now practise independently as Arkheion
Architects. A new-build scheme, Timber Wharf (2002),
designed by Glenn Howells Architects, was then inserted
between the two buildings along the edge of the

Bridgewater Canal. In the next year or so, Timber Wharf is to be further supplemented by Burton Place, also by Howells (50 out of the 90 units having already being sold off plan) and the proposed Mo-Ho by ShedKM, which is to be Urban Splash's first venture into prefabrication.

In Liverpool, Urban Splash's award-winning conversion of the Collegiate School (2001), also designed by ShedKM, contrasts a historic 19th-century Gothic facade with a modern rear elevation. Primarily loft dwellings, these kinds of schemes arguably cater for a very small portion of the housing market, with less than an eighth of householders in England living in flats and still smaller numbers in inner-city areas.[2] In terms of price and layout they are targeted at an even smaller section of society – relatively wealthy professionals without families, whether young or middle-aged. (Remaining two-bedroom flats at Box Works are being sold at various price points between £215,000 and £288,000, depending on size and outlook.)

However, it is Urban Splash's ability to feed and move with public taste that has made its influence extend far beyond its existing customer base. The large house-builders, who have the real potential to expand this market, have responded to Urban Splash by setting up their own city divisions. Whereas once local authorities were practically paying Bloxham to develop land, Urban Splash has almost been driven out of central Manchester by competition with its competitors and imitators for suitable sites.

To a certain degree the development of Urban Splash has been instinctive, moving in tandem with the cultural *Zeitgeist* while always maintaining a small critical step ahead. This has allowed it to anticipate people's needs and desires while not being too far out in front as to be out of sync. Largely brought up in south London, Bloxham originally came to Manchester in the early 1980s to study politics and modern history. It was a move that pre-empted Manchester in its students' heyday of the mid- to late 1980s. By the close of the decade, Hacienda may have been almost over, but Manchester was the only place to be. Stranded on a 1970s campus in East Anglia, I experienced the bright lights at second hand through brief weekend visits to friends; Manchester had become an international magnet for any student who was interested in clubbing or the music scene. It was a period that laid down the foundations for the city's regeneration, with bars and clubs opening up in the city centre to cater for the vital youth culture.

This intense nightlife and music scene provided an important catalyst for redevelopment, turning the tide on the massive depopulation experienced by Britain's northern cities in the 1970s. When Bloxham had finished with education in 1986, he catered for this market by setting up a business selling T-shirts and posters of bands such as The Smiths and New Order.[3]

To a certain degree the development of Urban Splash has been instinctive, moving in tandem with the cultural *Zeitgeist* while always maintaining a small critical step ahead. This has allowed it to anticipate people's needs and desires while not being too far out in front as to be out of sync.

Right
Interior and exterior of Timber Wharf, Manchester, designed by Glenn Howells Architects, completed July 2002. Howells won the commission to design this substantial scheme through the Britannia Basin European competition.

25

(His interest is still apparent in the show flats in Timber Wharf, where original Sex Pistols posters are framed on the walls.) Soon, however, Bloxham's inability to find suitable business premises for his market stall brought him into property. In 1987 he became the entrepreneur behind Affleck's Arcade, adjoining Affleck's Palace, a mixed-use market in the centre of Manchester that rented out spaces to small fashion outlets and record stalls, catering for the micro commerce that was being fuelled by Manchester's youth culture. But in 1991 his eyes were opened to the possibilities of design when he met the architect John Falkingham, who persuaded him to buy into Baa Bar, the restaurant-club he had designed in Liverpool.

In the early 1990s, Bloxham continued to consolidate his success at Affleck's Arcade by providing specialist shopping and managed work spaces at Liverpool Palace (1992) and Ducie House (1992) in Liverpool. But it was not until 1993, when Bloxham and Falkingham got together to found Urban Splash, that the company started to focus on an important gap in the market – city-centre living – and design became more of an issue. With Concert Square in Liverpool (1993 and 1995) and Sally's Yard Lofts (1995), the School House (1996) and Smithfield Buildings (1998) in Manchester, Urban Splash developed the first loft apartments in the North above commercial space to lease.

What made Urban Splash's success in the 1990s all the more remarkable was its patronage of local architects' offices in the Northwest and Midlands, giving major commissions to the likes of Stephenson Bell in Manchester, Glenn Howells Architects in Birmingham and Ian Simpson Architects in Manchester, all of which have since gone on to greatly expand their practices. The co-director of Urban Splash, Falkingham was the founder of Liverpool office Shed, which has since amalgamated with King McAllister to become ShedKM, and he clearly understood the abilities of other local offices.

At a grass-roots level, Urban Splash chose to work with architects who understood what Urban Splash was setting out to achieve culturally. Bloxham emphasises that so often the choice of architect is down to 'picking a team, rather than a scheme'. He was greatly impressed, for instance, by Howell's ability as a thinker and doer as well as a designer. When he enquired about fabricating a glass balustrade for Timber Wharf Howells was not stumped by a high quote; he went local and found someone who could produce it at half the cost. The quest, as Bloxham describes it, to create 'great buildings' at Urban Splash has made design integral to its schemes, as well as part of its customer's expectations. This reflects a true commitment on Bloxham's part, as Roger Stephenson of Stephenson Bell describes: 'The difference between Tom Bloxham and many other inner-city developers is that he believes in good design, seeks those who can deliver it and reaps the rewards from superior end products. Design for Tom is not a "bought in" added extra, but an integral part of the process.'

For the 2000s, it is clear that Bloxham is upping the ante; as he says, moving forward every couple of years

Right
ShedKM, the Collegiate School, Liverpool, 2001. The Victorian Gothic facade is decisively contrasted with a modern rear elevation.

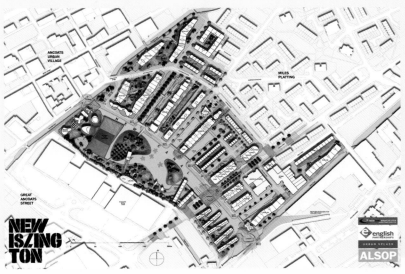

Alsop Architects, scheme for New Islington, Ancoats, Manchester.
Site plan and close-up of model, and existing boarded-up terrace at the Cardroom Estate, the site for the New Islington scheme. Waterways will be key to the area's new identity, not only making it an attractive place to live but bringing in people from outside to use its amenities. The Rochdale and Ashton canals that currently flank both sides of the site and require cleaning (they contain oil and pollutants from old adjacent industrial sites), will be linked by a new waterway. This new canal will divide the spaces between each development finger into distinctive localities. To prevent erosion of public space, Alsop's design is imbuing each area with a distinct purpose. While in some places the waterways will be given soft edging to create habitation for wildlife, in other areas they will be given hard banking for mooring and leisure use such as terraces for cafés. Additional focus will be supplied through the creation of facilities such as the orchard and 'Eco Island' that will be of educational use for schools as well as providing local beauty spots.

and reinventing himself has been part of the process – from market stall to Affleck's Palace, to small-scale mixed-use schemes to major loft developments. With its development of a substantial apartment complex at Royal William Yard in Plymouth, Urban Splash has made a bid to become a national company, appointing a managing director for operations in the Southwest in April 2003. It has also moved to another level in terms of the architects it appoints.

For its new scheme at Altrincham, a 292-apartment development just outside Manchester, Foster and Partners are constructing three new buildings. This is also Urban Splash's first site outside a city centre. At New Islington, Urban Splash is working with another leading London architectural firm, Alsop Architects, again outside the urban core of the city. But the magnitude of this project undertaken by the New East Manchester Urban Regeneration Company, in collaboration with English Partnerships, the city council and the local community, is far greater in terms of both area and regeneration. The New Islington Millennium Community (previously known as the Cardroom Estate) at Ancoats, in east

Manchester, covers a 10-hectare site and the intention is to build 1,400 new homes, offices and facilities. Since it was built in the 1970s, the existing suburban low-rise housing estate has experienced a steady 20-year decline and depopulation, which in recent years has left only half of the 204 homes occupied. This has made local services – shops, pubs and transport – unviable further escalating the sense of isolation and dereliction.

For New Islington, Alsop's office is undertaking its first urban framework study to really tackle residential issues, with the support of Urban Splash, which is also, aside from its small-scale scheme at Chorlton Park in Manchester (see 'New Designs in House Building: Interview with David Birkbeck of Design for Homes', in this issue), on new ground with the provision of mixed-tenure accommodation. Bloxham regards this as an opportunity to really turn around the way that housing is traditionally sold, by advocating the kind of flexible financial packages that are offered by car retailers. This would enable the lines between private and public (or housing association) ownership to become blurred, so that everyone buys into their home whatever the stake, the only difference between one occupant and the other being the degree of financial support they are able to obtain from their local housing association.

Notes
1. 'Concrete Boot', *Building
Design*, 14 March 2003.
2. David Birkbeck, 'How to
Home: Part 1', *7000 Words
on Housing*, RIBA, 2003.
3. For more on the cultural
context of the regeneration
of Manchester and Liverpool,
see Luke Bainbridge, 'A place
to live, work and play', in
'Cities Reborn', a special
supplement of *The Guardian*
produced in association with
English Partnership for the
Urban Summit (31 October–
1 November 2002), p 6.

Once again, though, for Bloxham and Alsop's office,
design is integral rather than a cosmetic afterthought.
As Christophe Egret from Alsop's states: 'Too often
urban design becomes wallpaper. Too often lazy
practitioners provide mood boards of some other place
that's nice. Too often there is too much analysis and
not enough vision. Fresh ideas and innovation must
and will be visible in everything we do.'

There is no question that working outside the city
centre, where there is an established market and an
infrastructure is in place, is playing to higher odds.
At this stage, Bloxham seems to be as resolved to be
as nimble and innovative in his operations as he has
been with urban loft dwellings. There are, however,
more restrictions and external constraints and more
compromises demanded at every stage. There are
some indications that Bloxham is remaining in tune
with the times, as the Planning Policy Guidance Note
3 (PPG3) is encouraging property developers and house
builders to employ architects (see 'New Designs in
House Building', opposite) and create housing at urban
densities in the suburbs and on urban extensions.
It just remains to be seen whether Bloxham has
been able to anticipate the next move in property
development or if this is a step too far. ⚙

New Designs in House Building: Interview with David Birkbeck of Design for Homes

In the last few years an uncharted revolution has been occurring in house building in the UK. A pioneering group of volume house builders, developers and housing associations has begun to realise the potential of design and employ architects on private and social housing schemes. In this interview with **Helen Castle**, David Birkbeck, chief executive of the campaigning and research body Design for Homes, explains that this is a pragmatic rather than aesthetic shift. In response to a shortage of land and new statutory guidelines, there is an increasing demand for architects with urban and spatial planning skills to design housing on brownfield and suburban sites.

Chorlton Park Apartments, Manchester, 2002

This block of flats was designed by Manchester practice Stephenson Bell for Irwell Valley Housing Association. Built on the site of a disused and badly contaminated former petrol station, the adjoining area is made up of two-storey semidetached houses and small shops. The local planners were supportive of Stephenson Bell's distinctive and landmark design, recognising the need for a high-quality design in an undistinguished suburban area. Originally planned by the housing association as 20 units, the involvement of Tom Bloxham of Urban Splash in the scheme as a joint developer enlarged the project to 27 units – four duplex apartments top the originally conceived block with a fourth and fifth storey. An underground car park was also added that uses the excavation from contamination.

Top right and page 29
Chorlton Park Apartments, Manchester, 2002. East-facing main elevation on the Barlow Moor Road with the first three floors of Irwell Housing Association apartments and the top two floors of duplex apartments.

Above
Chorlton Park Apartments. East-facing main elevation on the Barlow Moor Road.

Right
At the rear of the apartments access balconies overlook a courtyard garden.

In the popular press, the allure of employing an architect on a project is perceived mainly in cosmetic terms. As design for design's sake it is presented as a lifestyle choice or a modern form of conspicuous consumption. This is perhaps largely a response to make-over shows and the successful urban loft developments of the 1990s, which marketed famous designers like Sir Terence Conran and Philippe Starck as brands. Design for Homes, a not-for-profit organisation that champions the value of good design in the residential industry and incorporates the Design for Homes Architects group, which is RIBA's official linked society for architects in the residential sector, has evolved a much more far-reaching vision for architects' involvement in house design; the emphasis being on mass housing rather than one-off signature homes.

David Birkbeck highlights the broader benefits of employing design consultancies on housing schemes, in terms of the potential quality of the total spaces they might afford and the economic rewards to the developer: 'Design for Homes believes – at the heart of what it stands for – that there is a real commercial value to the development of streets and residential developments generally in the best possible way, but we don't necessarily associate that directly with the quality of the architectural detail. We're more interested in the packaging of space both in and around the new properties – what they now call place-making: the general amenity that you can ease into a development nowadays if you design enough living space, do obvious things like specify enough storage and focus on how the buildings will present together.

'We promote and campaign for the most generous developments, for the advantages offered to the people who live in them and for the enduring appeal of these places. We know that space is the single most powerful determinant of whether a scheme is sustainable – if it skimps, occupants will always be looking to move on. We can prove with our own research that well-designed developments are better for the landlord housing association that procures them because they tend to be the developments that increase in value among their portfolio. And for house builders in the market sale sector, although it may require a more complicated procurement process initially, designs by architects in tune with what the market wants invariably catch up with a typical programme by selling at a much increased rate and also at increased prices.'

Birkbeck believes that the critical catalyst for the change in the mindset of house builders and developers, who traditionally relied on national house-types for 90 per cent or more of build, is brownfield development: 'Historically, house builders always sold on location – the site that was closest to the good school or had access to the motorway, or was near to the train station. It was as simple as that. Whatever was sold would sell at as much as a 30 or 40 per cent premium over the traditional property in the area because it was a spanking new building and, ideally, situated for the best facilities in the area. Now, a lot of those locations were edge-to-town locations, the scrubland that is often sententiously referred to as "greenfield". The developers chose which part of the limits of existing development they wanted to build on, and when they succeeded in getting that site adopted by the local planning authority potentially they were selling in a monopoly situation, usually being the only new build in that area.

'But government accelerated a shift to brownfield with its sequential approach to new sites being adopted in local plans: many previously undeveloped sites cannot be adopted for the time being until local authorities can prove they have exhausted the potential of sites within the developed zones. This said to the building developers: "No, you can't choose any more where the location is; the local authority now decides and it will select the areas it wants regenerated first, second, third and last. And not only will you not be able to choose the site that's closest to the school that you want to be able to market as part of the amenities, but you will also be right next door to all your other house-builder friends, because you're all going to be operating from roughly similar sites in roughly similar locations – and they may even all be the wrong side of town."

'That's where house builders had to analyse whether they want to sell their products on lowest price. They basically compete – "our units cost £85k and their units cost £90k". No developer likes to sell on price, because the risk is that they end up cutting each other's throats in order to sell when the market turns down. The alternative model is differentiation: they sell on the fact that they've got special qualities to the development. This is generally the planning of space and the security of the environment, which can be designed to be secure even when the postcode suggests otherwise. Remember the recent national census where issues of security topped the public's concerns? House builders are looking to consultants to plan spaces for greater amenity and greater security, even if their site is on the wrong side of the tracks. That was where the origins of the involvement with architects came from, and increasingly over the last couple of years the actual building envelope itself and the qualities of the building in terms of architecture have come more into play. Rising property values have allowed developers to spend more money on the quality of the buildings themselves, and they have also been learning how to manage the risk of the nonstandard approach. As they get more confident, the designs become more expansive.'

The sequential approach is just one part of what Birkbeck says has been the catalyst for most change in recent years – PPG3, the Planning Policy Guidance Note 3 on housing. He maintains that although this statutory guidance is widely known first for acting as a density threshold, it is now functioning as a design threshold: 'It's possible to get schemes built in this country that are below PPG3 densities provided that the design is good enough. It is

designers to get the maximum value out of what they're going to build by maintaining design quality as the massing on a site climbs.' This, Birkbeck explains, greatly contrasts with the situation that existed prior to PPG3. The earlier set of guidelines that Michael Hesseltine produced in 1980 as Secretary of State for the Environment was aimed at reducing red tape and placing power in the hands of the private sector. Decision-making on design was to be 'the prerogative of housebuilders marketing personnel ... in the light of their customers requirements' rather than of local government officers. This situation was completely reversed by PPG3, which in paragraph 67 outrightly invites planners to become concerned with the quality of design, instructing them to reject poor design.

What is PPG3?

Planning Policy Guidance Note 3 is a radical statutory guidance issued by central government in March 2000 to all planning authorities in order to limit the number of detached properties being built on previously developed land.

Its four objectives can be described as:
- Increasing the volume of new homes released from each development, by introducing (previously unimagined) minimum-density thresholds designed to squeeze 20 to 50 per cent more homes from each site, often by promoting urban brownfield sites at the expense of lower density rural greenfield sites;
- Replacing five- and six-bedroom detached properties with more flats or smaller houses (to deal with the forecastthat of four million additional households due to form by 2016, 80 per cent will be people living alone);
- Reducing the amount of development land dedicated to car parking (which averaged 38 per cent) by limiting on-plot parking to 1.5 spaces on average across any planning proposal;
- Promoting better design through demands that all planning proposals take account of good practice, not least in addressing local materials, local landscape and local landmark buildings (shadowing criteria more strictly employed in conservation areas).

increasingly difficult to get schemes through that are above the PPG3 threshold but are of poor design.' He cites planning appeals in Chelmsford and Redditch. The former rejected a scheme above the density threshold on the grounds of poor design quality, the latter allowed an appeal for a scheme below the density threshold on the grounds that design quality should be allowed to overrule density standards. Birkbeck points out that PPG3 now requires 'applicants to demonstrate how they have considered good design', obliging applicants to identify where designs sat in the procurement process.

In some local planning authorities, identifying the involvement of architects is often regarded as a prerequisite to planning: 'Some house builders and developers are using designers to get schemes through in sensitive areas where they would like to develop the largest possible houses at the lowest density. Conversely others are using

For clarification, poor design is defined and identified. It is, for instance, associated with monocultural development (the rows of executive boxes that Hesseltine's 1980 circular unleashed). With an emphasis on sustainable mixed communities, which incorporate local amenities and businesses, the design is again not in the detail but in the whole.

Though Birkbeck admits that from a marketing point of view the press coverage of 'boutique operations' such as Manhattan Lofts and Urban Splash may have had some impact on customers' aspirations and tastes, real change has had to come from within the residential industry itself. Among volume house builders, inner-city loft dwellings are regarded as a niche market. For a broader confidence in the benefits of design within their own sector, property developers and house builders require commercial precedents and pioneers in their own field: 'The thing that makes the industry change its heart is the volume house-builders who actually do some of this for themselves. Once people who procure those major developments don't lose their jobs, they actually get promoted. That's the real change in the industry. Every now and again, people have risen quite quickly up the ladder in the housing companies on the grounds that they have been more experimental and have been able to manage the risk.'

Despite the predominance of large national house-building firms in the UK, the approach to development remains surprisingly unstandardised. Thus advances remain piecemeal with, as Birkbeck explains, pockets of progress focused around specific regional offices:

'The problem with the volume house-builders is that you might have a company that has a dozen regional offices, and there might be a regional director in the Southwest who knows how to do this, but it doesn't mean that across the whole house-building operation they can all do it. Take for example Ronnie Baird who was managing director at Wimpey Homes North East. Baird did not like building national house-types. He would do anything but national house-types. You should see what he did with the Wills Building. He took a factory in the Northeast by the main Newcastle-upon-Tyne road, which is really a horrible piece of urban planning. It's enormous – a great big, hulking Art Deco factory. It had remained empty and been a derelict building for something like 25 years. When I went to visit my grandparents in the area, it was the building that all the 11-year-olds in the area would vandalise on an afternoon. All I remember was that it was just there and everybody used to think it was a disgrace. There were about five or six wacky ideas for what it might become in the 1980s, when there was lots of money flashing around. Then just at the very point where the council was about to demolish it, Ronnie Baird stepped in and bought it, and he converted it into residential accommodation.'

Baird was also responsible for regenerating North Shields with his schemes for Bankside and Union Square. His ability for a fresh approach meant that when Wayne Hemingway, the co-founder of Red or Dead fashion brand, approached Keith Cushen, chairman of Wimpey Homes, with the idea of collaborating on a project, Cushion directed him to Baird, who was now managing director of George Wimpey City. Hemingway's involvement with the Staiths South Bank scheme in Gateshead has brought it a substantial amount of attention in the popular press, and on TV Hemingway has now become the voice for housing, outside the industry. Though Staiths South Bank is being designed by Mark Massey from Ian Darby Partnership, the scheme is centred on the ideas of Hemingway and his partner Gerardine, for housing that engenders a sense of community and social ownership with communal courtyard gardens and car-free roads. They have also advocated a layout that places the bedrooms on the ground floor and the living spaces on the first floor. A choice of colourful facades allows for a certain amount of customisation of individual properties and allows people to identify their own homes within the whole.

Despite Baird's involvement with this high-profile project, Birkbeck emphasises that where Baird really proved himself was on bespoke schemes like the Wills Building where he became 'a specialist in making land values out of places where there are none. Turning some kind of nightmare of a negative value into a positive proposal by getting a design that completely obliterates the memory of the place.'

Just how instrumental high-quality design can be for long-term regeneration is clearly understood by the Peabody Trust in London. Whereas in the 1990s, local authorities and housing associations were often pulling down the relatively unsuccessful architectural statements of the 1960s and replacing them with quite poorly detailed buildings – something Birkbeck describes as 'anywhere, any place' architecture – it was soon realised that however pleased the residents were in the short term to have a brand-new home, this approach did not inspire a great sense of community because the new homes often had a poor sense of place or identity and so did not become a desirable new address. Consequently, the Peabody Trust is now building a tower into many of its regeneration bids, as a physical signpost to a new address. Thus, Birkbeck explains: 'They let it be known that they're going to sell some expensive flats in this tower which is going to become a symbol for the confidence of this regeneration project. That's the way they say to everyone in the area: "You thought this was just another run-down estate not worth a second look. Well, look at this! Here's a 14-storey apartment block, clad in colourful modern materials, and though its mixed tenure, some people will pay as much as £500 a square foot to live in it."'

The successful mixture of private and public housing is a finely honed skill of design and development. In Birkbeck's words, it takes architects who, with a bespoke solution, 'are able to do something pretty special with the design'. As he points out: 'How do you get people to pay £350,000 for a flat when some of the housing associations' tenants in the same building will have their rents paid for as state benefits? One set of people have got Audi TTs, while the other set have got a car with an F-plate reg.' The rewards can, of course, be high for housing associations as this mix provides them with a line of cross-subsidy that often enables them to produce higher quality housing for their tenants and more valuable stock. However, this also represents a calculated risk dependent on the housing market and a very confident scheme. One such case is Chorlton Park in Manchester, where the design was so enticing that a private developer actually asked to come on board. Tom Bloxham of Urban Splash, who was one of the judges for Irwell Valley Housing Association on the design competition, was so impressed with Stephenson Bell's proposal that he persuaded Irwell Valley to re-engineer the project to include a further floor of apartments that could be sold by Urban Splash as private penthouses. Chorlton Park is all the more remarkable for its success in that the architects ran the job under a conventional JCT (Joint Contracts Tribunal) contract. It is also not located in the centre of a city where the blurring of private and public is often less conspicuous, but in a suburban area of Manchester.

For Birkbeck, it is in suburbia that the greatest impact of PPG3 and a new approach to planning and design is to be felt. Whereas UK towns have conventionally followed a pyramid principle with eight to ten storeys in the centre and one to two storeys at the outer edge, the insistence on higher densities is bringing about a scale of three or four storeys in out-of-town areas. This is a development, he points out, that is akin to the 19th-century Edinburgh New Town, where town houses of three to four storeys were built at the edge of the city. The effect is to be felt not only on building heights but also in the pattern and layout of streets. Whereas suburbs have conventionally grown up off distributor roads with feeder roads and cul-de-sacs, containing closes of family houses or generously laid out areas of executive homes, 'like a trunk, branch and twig', suburban streets are now being planned on American-style grids – the main streets being laid out like broad boulevards with trees down the middle. This allows for a four- or five-storey frontage with shops at the bottom. Large parts of Swindon and Northampton are being developed in this manner. Building these big boulevards is lucrative for the developers as, unless they want to look badly planned, the frontages on the main road have to be pushed up to at least four storeys. This all means more residential space to sell as well as commercial leasings; whereas they used to get 12,000 feet to the acre they can now get 30,000, an increase that also affords developers the luxury of architects' fees.

An award-winning example of this approach, which embraces PPG3, is Newhall in Harlow, Essex (for images see Rob Wilson, 'Common Ground', in this issue). This is a greenfield site that has been developed on an urban scale with 43 dwellings on a hectare. Built by Copthorn Homes Ltd, which is part of Countryside Properties plc, it was designed by Proctor and Matthews Architects and is one of 10 packages of land earmarked for development and thus adheres to a greater master plan for the area created by Roger Evans Associates for local landowners, the Moen family. One of the main features of the site is the corner towers, which provide not only higher density housing but also act as landmark buildings for the area. There is a great deal of variety in type and height within the site, with four or five medium-rise storeys at the front and lower-rise mews houses around the mews courtyards. Flexibility is also built into the larger houses, creating possibilities for converting the basements into work units. The whole scheme has a strong identity with contemporary colours as well as the introduction of local materials such as thatch. Birkbeck sums it up: 'This is a greenfield extension between Harlow and the M11, typifying the old style of land release where you would expect a standardised layout of large mock-Tudor homes. But what are they trying to do instead? They're building a glamorous extension, urban in form, to the town of Harlow, with proper boulevards and landmark buildings and a serious attempt to update Essex's famous vernacular.'

For all intents and purposes Newhall is an exceptional scheme. This is largely because of the interest of the landowners whose insistence on creating a high-quality environment led them to invite tenders by interviewing developer/architects teams and selecting the best design/bid. It may be unusual but it is also indicative of the way that current land shortages in the UK have been able to squeeze the residential industry in such a way as to make quality in terms of planning and space a new priority. As Birkbeck concludes, the potential for architects in housing, 'shouldn't just be seen as designers winning the battle. Opportunities for designers have been created by changes in the statutory guidance, by the shortage of land and by the brand-new focus, which suddenly meant that instead of being window dressing on apartment blocks, design is now being used in its original manner. We're now right back with the 18th-century idea of what architects and urban planners do.'

Design for Homes produces regular seminars introducing consultant architects and their ideas for residential planning and design to members of the House Builders Federation, the members of which jointly produce 80 per cent of the UK's 165,000 new homes each year. The current series will run to the end of 2003 and is sponsored by English Partnerships, the national regeneration agency. Consultants wishing to take part should enrol in Design for Homes Architects Group by posting details about their practice in our directory of consultants, www.architectsearch.co.uk, which is subsidised by Design for Homes.

launched in August 2002, the trust claims to have one of the 'most ambitious strategies for sustainability in the social and affordable housing sector'. However, in recent years it has also marked itself out by using its very special position as a general charity committed to the relief of poverty in London to spearhead the application of new construction technologies, specifically prefabrication. This strategy has been backed up by the recommendations of the 1998 Egan Report, which highlighted the declining supply of skilled labour and the need to reduce wastage in the construction industry, recommending house builders take new approaches.

In 1998 Peabody placed itself at the forefront of the move towards off-site construction with its development of Murray Grove in Hackney, London, designed by Cartwright Pickard. Adopting a modular housing system, it used prefabricated steel (the modules were steel-framed) housing units that were fully equipped with

Peabody Trust

Director of development Dickon Robinson says of Murray Grove: 'It has been a huge success both in terms of promoting a new form of construction and in the design of the building, which has won many architectural and engineering awards. We're now applying what we've learnt about volumetric construction to create a residential bridge structure at Trinity Buoy Wharf at the mouth of the River Lea.'

Above top
Construction shots of prefabricated units being assembled at Raines Court in Stoke Newington, London, designed by Allford, Hall, Monaghan and Morris.

Above bottom
As the largest scale prefabricated housing scheme in the country at the time it was built, Murray Grove in Hackney, London, has had a tremendous impact on house builders and housing associations as well as on the architectural community.

The Peabody Trust
In 1862, the American-born philanthropist George Peabody founded the Peabody Donation Fund, which defined the trust's objectives as 'the construction of such dwellings for the poor as may combine in the utmost degree the essentials of healthfulness, comfort, social enjoyment and economy' for Londoners. Though the trust's mission to 'ameliorate the conditions of the poor and needy of London' remains the same today, an emphasis on high-quality social housing has allowed it, as one of the capital's largest housing associations, to take a pioneering role in the construction of housing. With over 19,000 homes across the city, its programme crosses 27 boroughs. Offering housing for outright sale, and shared ownership as well as cost rent, it aims to provide for a broad range of residents through a scheme of flexible financial packages, while also using the funds raised from outright sales to cross-subsidise affordable rented housing.

With ecologically engineered schemes, such as BedZED designed by Bill Dunster Architects, and its comprehensive Sustainability Strategy

plumbing, electrics, doors, windows, bathroom and kitchen fittings, tiles and carpets. To ensure the scheme's success architecturally, provision was made for fine detailing and materials. A corner glass lift-tower also provided an urban marker or centrepiece to the scheme. In order to recover a substantial percentage of the cost of Murray Grove, the apartments were made available at cost rent for those who do not generally qualify for social housing but would be unable to afford market rents or a mortgage in London.

Also in Hackney, the trust is now developing a second modular scheme with Allford, Hall, Monaghan and Morris as architects. Raines Court in Stoke Newington will consist of 53 shared-ownership flats, targeted at key workers and local people, with eight live/work units on the open market. Using a system manufactured by Yorkon, the aim is to improve on the speed and efficiency of the prefabricated construction championed at Murray Grove.

At Goldsmiths Close in Ealing, west London, Peabody is currently working with Arup Associates on Project Meteor, which aims this time to utilise the potential of precast concrete to create a flexible off-site prefabricated system.

Ronnie Baird

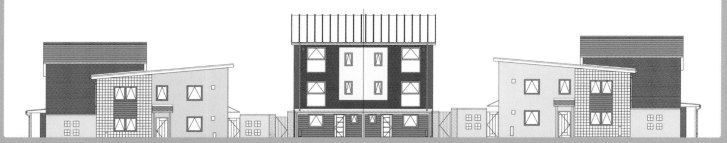

Above bottom
Ronnie Baird on site at Union Square in North Shields.

Above top
Elevation of town houses at Staiths South Bank, Gateshead.

Opposite, top
Assael's design for the Great Northern Tower. In a prime location in central Manchester, this landmark tower is set for completion in 2005.

Opposite, bottom left
Illustration of the Staiths South Bank scheme, Gateshead, designed by Wayne and Gerardine Hemingway in collaboration with Ian Darby Partnership, showing the focus that has been given to communal shared space in the planning of the scheme.

Opposite, bottom right
The refurbished Wills Building on the coast road leading into Newcastle has become a symbol of the city's regeneration. A 1940s factory, built in the 1930s Art Deco style, it was a major employer in the area until its closure and dereliction in the mid-1980s.

Ronnie Baird
Managing Director of George Wimpey City

Having worked for George Wimpey for 13 years, Ronnie Baird is an innovator working from the inside of the house-building industry. As managing director of Wimpey Homes North East between 1994 and 2001, he successfully spearheaded bespoke development within the group from a regional division. Converting properties as diverse as Wylam Manor in Northumberland, the Art Deco Wills Factory in Newcastle, Ayton Friends Development in North Yorkshire and the historical Wilton Castle on Teesside, Wimpey North East also regenerated brownfield sites such the North Shields Union Square scheme by Jane Darbyshire and David Kendall.

Internally and externally, Ronnie Baird's brave but sound commercial development solutions in the Northeast have been rewarded: in October 2001, Baird was appointed Managing Director of George Wimpey City, a new division of Wimpey that was set up to create prestigious city-centre developments outside London. Current ones include sites on Newcastle Quayside, Cardiff, central Manchester and Edinburgh. His service to architecture has also been acknowledged by the design community with his appointment by the Commission for Architecture and the Built Environment (CABE) as an Architectural Champion for 2001/2002.

Though Baird set out a strategy in 1996/7 to significantly increase bespoke developments in the Northeast, he is careful to explain that this was not from a baseline position: 'There has been a very long history of building bespoke developments by Wimpey in the Northeast. In the late 1980s, Wimpey was developing apartments on York riverside, in the 1990s we developed Victoria Lock in Teesdale (which won the best brownfield development site in England award from English Heritage in 1999). I arrived in the Northeast for Wimpey in 1994 having previously been involved with apartment developments in Edinburgh and the east of Scotland.'

Currently working on such high-profile schemes as the Great Northern Tower in Manchester by Assael, and Staiths South Bank in Gateshead designed by Ian Darby Partnership in collaboration with Wayne and Gerardine Hemingway, the co-founders of the Red or Dead fashion brand, Baird is well aware of the benefits of good design, whether as an aid to planning on a difficult brownfield site or on a greenfield site with increased densities 'to ensure a sense of community is created with a sense of place and an attractive environment'. There is also, of course, the need as a home producer to cater for the ever-evolving market and the requirements of the buyers: 'Home buyers are becoming more design savvy; whether it is interior trends or architect-designed schemes, there is tremendous interest in well-thought-out, well-designed concepts.'

Baird is aided at George Wimpey City by development director Ian Laight who has already had a very successful career as an architect with his own practice. Laight is responsible for developing the concept of the schemes, briefing the architects and managing the developments through all planning and technical approval processes. Architects are carefully matched to housing schemes and selected for particular skills, whether these are the ability to sensitively maximise the potential of a historic conversion or produce a stunning modern flagship building on a waterfront. The creative has to always be tempered with economic requirements. As Baird states: 'From my perspective, the most important aspect is that architects must have a passion for what they want to build but not lose sight of the commercial realities.'

Copthorn Homes

Above
Show apartment, designed
by Conran Design Group for
Woodrange House (formerly
West Five Studios), Ealing,
London, 2002.

Opposite, top left and
bottom right
Proctor and Matthews, Mile
End Road, London, 2001.

Opposite, bottom left
Proctor and Matthews and
Erskine Tovatt, Becquerel
Court at Greenwich Millennium
Village, 2003. This second
phase of the millennium
village consists of 186 units of
three-bedroom houses, one-
and two-bedroom apartments
and live/work units. The
Greenwich Millennium Village
demonstrates Copthorn's and
Countryside's spearheading
of successful partnerships.
It is a joint venture between
Countryside Properties and
Taylor Woodrow Developments
Ltd in association with English
Partnerships.

Opposite, top right and
middle right
Four-bedroom E-type town
house designed by Proctor and
Matthews for Newhall, Essex,
completed 2003. The E-type
house includes a flexible
ground-floor space that builds
in a certain amount of flexibility
of use, allowing the occupants
to partition it off into a
separate work or living area.

Copthorn Homes

A division of Countryside Properties plc, Copthorn Homes was founded in 1994 by the group's chairman, Alan Cherry, and chief executive Graham Cherry. Set up to cater for first-time buyers, it has since established a reputation for delivering innovative, high-quality homes on brownfield sites and urban extensions that are sensitive to the environment. In the 2002 Housing Design Awards, its development at Mile End Road, designed by Proctor and Matthews Architects, received the Building for Life Award, and its Newhall scheme at Harlow in Essex, in which the architects were also Proctor and Matthews, received the House-Builder Award.

This architectural success comes from the group's use of bespoke design solutions at every one of its developments and its commitment to corporate social responsibility. As Alan Cherry states: 'Delivering profitability with sustainability is one of our core values. We are totally committed to innovative, responsible development. It creates added value and opens up new business opportunities that should in turn lead to superior financial performance.'

Imaginative planning and design certainly aid developers such as Countryside Properties to secure planning consents in the wake of PPG3, which overtly states that local planning authorities should 'reject poor design'. Copthorn, however, also acknowledges that at a time of land shortages, design quality encourages landowners and local planning authorities to set up vital partnerships with them. This is certainly the case at Newhall where they had to put together a competitive tender with Proctor and Matthews, which was selected principally for its design quality by the landowners.

At Copthorn Homes there is also a broader recognition that good housing design has become much desired by its customers. As Dave DeVries, design director of Copthorn Homes, explains: 'Design is an important ingredient where bespoke solutions are required for each development. A focus is required on an individual basis to achieve quality for the community, and meet people's aspirations not only for quality living but also for quality design. This will give added value to properties in this designer age, as can be seen in so many fashionable things such as clothes, furniture and cars.' Δ

Common Ground:

Mediating Thresholds Between Public and Private Space in UK Housing Design

Rob Wilson traces how over the last two decades British society's increasingly narcissistic tendency – revealed by its emphasis on privatisation and the self – have effectively eroded the accommodation of both public and threshold spaces in housing. In the wake of the Urban Task Force and PPG3, he looks at three projects that have reversed this trend, injecting a sense of ownership into shared spaces.

An increasing disjuncture between the private and the public realms – or what we perceive as the space of our personal lives and then everything else – has long been observed, particularly in relation to the design of the built environment, and notably in Richard Sennett's *The Fall of Public Man* (1977).[1] Here, the origins of this trend are traced, primarily in Western and capitalist societies, to a growing belief that in our private lives we are seeking a reflection of our inner psyches and what is 'authentic' in our feelings. This in turn means that anything seen as impersonal – traditionally public life – is increasingly perceived as something of no value and meaningless, effecting:'the effacement of the *res publica* by the belief that social meanings are generated by the feelings of individual human beings.'[2]

Sennett argues that this increasing state of what he terms 'narcissism' has affected key areas of our social life, including an increased understanding of our homes as reflections of ourselves.

In the quarter-century since the publication of Sennett's book, all the evidence suggests that this tendency has reached new peaks. Whilst in the media and politics, validity is sought through the personal experiences of journalists and politicians, so day-to-day we seek self-validation in the personal space we create around

ourselves. On the back of a continuing consumer boom, clothes, furniture, food and living space have all been co-opted in the belief pattern of lifestyle as core value, reinforced by home make-over and cooking shows on TV.

And in magazines such as *Wallpaper**, with its by-line 'the stuff that surrounds you', our personal lives are presented as capable of co-opting the whole world in an unlimited extension of ego, treating it as a consumable item – a global mirror of our idealised sense of self.

Ultimately, though, back in the lived world it is the physical stuff of architecture and building that has to mediate this disjuncture between public and private and provide a literal threshold. And architecture not only divides but defines and makes explicit this threshold: 'Architects ... are among the few professionals who are forced to work with present-day ideas of public life ... who of necessity express and make these codes manifest to others.'[3]

In the built environment nothing presents a greater challenge than housing, providing for the most intimate events of people's lives whilst engaging with the public realm at its most fluid and informal: the residential area. And in this void of meaning and excess of aspiration today, housing is back on the agenda in the UK. The need is huge, with between 3.8 and 4.4 million more households predicted to form over the next 25 years, fuelled perhaps by this very 'narcissism': 80 per cent of projected household growth is due to an increase in single-person households – more people opting to be alone in their own self-reflective space. (A trend already

Opposite
Coin Street, South Bank, London SE1, 2000–01.
Private gardens directly access the courtyard.

Coin Street, South Bank, London SE1, 2000–01)
Architect: Haworth Tompkins Architects
Client: Coin Street Community Builders
Number of units: 59
Density: 334 habitable rooms per hectare
(Lambeth Local Unitary Development
Plan recommendation: 210 per hectare)

Consisting of primarily three- and four-bedroom town houses with 18 maisonettes and nine apartments, this scheme forms the perimeter to three sides of a block on a very busy inner-urban situation, the fourth side of which is due to be completed by a neighbourhood centre.

Rising to five storeys, the northern and longest perimeter has retail corner units at ground level and combines three-storey town houses topped by apartments and maisonettes, which are accessed from a gated lift and stairwell giving glimpses into the courtyard. The hard threshold to the street is fronted by bin stores, backed neatly on to the public pavement, with a raised access walkway running behind serving recessed gated porches that contain storage and are surveyed by the kitchen window. This 'privacy gradient', as the architects describe it, is repeated less successfully due to a lack of level change on the shorter though less busy sides of the block, formed by the four-storey town houses.

The scheme frames an internal courtyard, 60 metres wide by 57 metres long, sitting over a commercial underground car park that subsidises the scheme. Every unit has either balconies or terraces overlooking the courtyard, and additionally each house has a 7-metre-deep private garden directly accessing the courtyard – the architects cite the latter arrangement as inspired by 19th-century models such as that seen at Stanley Gardens in Notting Hill Gate.

Underlining the public/private divide provided by the block itself, the severe brick street facade is strongly contrasted with a sustainable hardwood timber rain-screen cladding of the courtyard facade, already weathering unevenly to a silvery grey.

The whole scheme is run by a cooperative of the tenants who vote on everything from imposing a 9pm courtyard curfew on under-18s to the inauguration of a weeding rota. The residents therefore have a level of control and thus a sense of ownership of their shared spaces, empowering them to adapt these to their changing needs.

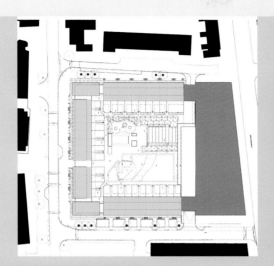

Coin Street, South Bank, London SE1, 2000–01

Opposite
Street facade showing how the bin stores and a change of level create an effective 'privacy gradient' from pavement to front door.

Top left
Block plan showing the layout of the threshold zone on the street and the inner courtyard.

Top right
Communal courtyard.

Middle
View down to the courtyard.

Right
Access terrace for the third-floor maisonettes, which residents are beginning to use, especially in the summer, as an extension of their living spaces.

reflected in the balance of accommodation in schemes such as that at Tilbury in Essex – see later.)

This growth, given existing pressure on land, will lead to increased housing densities already reflected in planning guidance documents such as PPG3. And higher densities mean more pressure on the common parts and thresholds that people share – and their design. In this it is useful to look at past models.

In most Victorian terraces, front gardens act as simple but defined threshold zones, often supplemented by a raised ground-floor and semi-basement. This achieves a delicate balance between privacy and engagement – of removal from, yet representation on, the street, a controlled but accessible semiprivate buffer zone.

> Over the last 50 years, the vital mediation provided by such threshold space has often been dissipated by designers due to a central tenet of Modernism – Cartesian 'free' space. This has led to a biasing towards object-based buildings over perimeter block developments, resulting in the loss of streets acting as definers of exterior space and a clearly legible public realm.

Over the last 50 years, the vital mediation provided by such threshold space has often been dissipated by designers due to a central tenet of Modernism – Cartesian 'free' space. This has led to a biasing towards object-based buildings over perimeter block developments, resulting in the loss of streets acting as definers of exterior space and a clearly legible public realm. The effect has been particularly significant in the UK, with its tradition of terraced houses and not apartments, as conceptually the exterior space of the street acted as an extension of the defining place of individual homes – terraces are not read as horizontal housing blocks.

As the Urban and Economic Development Group (Urbed) has observed: 'Today the street tends to be seen as a means of gaining access to a site whereas in traditional cities streets were the way in which boundaries of sites were defined.'[4] The desirability of streets as defining thresholds has rarely been in question. It underlined Alison and Peter Smithson's attempt to naturalise and break down the Corbusian block by creating 'streets-in-the-air' within it, pulling horizontal circulation to its edges in an effort to create 'places and not corridors or balconies ... [where] ... the refuse chute takes the place of the village pump'.[5] Such aspirations for these 'streets' now seem almost tragically misplaced, in practice often further confusing

residents' ability to identify the private and public realms around their dwellings – the fusion of walkway and threshold muddying any sense of ownership (although subsequent maintenance and management failures also contributed).

In terms of density, too, with its implications for privacy and overlooking, terraces again provide an interesting model for higher-density housing. Often built with significantly less than 10 metres between overlooking windows, compared with most local authority unitary development policy recommendations of a 20-metre minimum, the environment of terraced or perimeter block schemes does not feel uncomfortable, and these still prove popular places in which to live – witness Haworth Tompkins's Housing Development at Coin Street. This is due to the defined but intimate certainties of the public/private divide from the street and the evident but limited area of surveillance afforded to each dwelling. In contrast, in Modernist schemes the underlying but irreconcilable ideal is of each person in his or her own panopticon, raised up on piloti, afforded space and light, and with a liberated but controlling gaze over his or her surroundings, simultaneously fully observing but unobserved. Such a concept, whilst unattainable, also casts the gaze of the Other in necessarily adversarial terms, meaning that even the potentially benign gaze of a neighbour becomes obtrusive.

Thus the surrounding landscaped space of many housing estates is experienced not just as an undifferentiated degraded threshold for which no one feels ownership but as an actively hostile place, its only definition being that it is not 'street'.

Architects have long tried to design out this *horror vacui*, as Neave Brown neatly summed up in an article about his own housing projects: 'All these schemes occupy their sites entirely. Nowhere is there any residual or unallocated space ...The typical void represents a conceptual void, an absence of purpose and an inability to recognize important needs.'[6]

Of course much of the design and planning of housing developments has been driven by the increasingly ubiquitous presence of the car and the understandable reaction to try to separate road user from pedestrian as much as possible. Hence 'streets-in-the-air', but also the low-rise estates of the 1970s based on the Radburn principles – housing laid out around vehicular cul-de-sacs and sometimes labyrinthine pedestrian walkways and alleys, named after the town in New Jersey, US, where a system of segregating cars and pedestrians developed by Clarence Stein was implemented for the first time. Both these forms of housing created either redundant space or that which lacks natural surveillance, which proved to provide perfect loci for vandalism and other criminal activity. The evidence, from studies such as those published on-line by Space

Notes
1. Richard Sennett, *The Fall of Public Man*, Faber and Faber (London), 1986.
2. Ibid, p 339.
3. Ibid, p 12.
4. David Rudlin and Nicholas Falk (Urbed), *Building the 21st Century Home: the Sustainable Urban Neighbourhood*, Architectural Press (London), 1999, p 178.
5. Peter Smithson on their designs for the Golden Lane Estate, 1952. Alison and Peter Smithson, *The Charged Void: Architecture*, The Monacelli Press (New York), 2001, p 86.
6. Neave Brown, 'Alexandra Road, Fleet Road, Winscombe Street', *Architecture and Urbanism*, 1, No 122, November 1980, p 4.
7. Joanna Averley and Mairi Johnson, 'Desirable densities', *Building Design*, 29 November 2002, pp 16–17.
8. Professor Bill Hillier, 'Crime and Space Research: the Need for Rigour', Space Syntax, www.spacesyntax.com/housing.
9. Interview with Margaret Thatcher for *Woman's Own*, 3 October 1987.
10. Based on the Parker Morris Report 'Homes for Today and Tomorrow', published 1961, with its recommendations for minimum levels of internal space, standards which became mandatory for all public-sector housing between 1967 and 1969. These standards were abolished in 1981 following the 1980 Local Government, Planning and Land Act. See the *Architects' Journal*, 17 November 1982, 'Can we afford not to have housing standards?' (p 39) and 'Housing Update' (p 69).
11. 'Rethinking Construction', published July 1998, produced by Sir John Egan's Construction Task Force for the then Department of Trade and Industry, looked at the scope for improving the quality and efficiency of UK construction.
12. Press release, 31 October 2002.
13. From the website www.homezonenews.org.uk.
14. Gordon Cullen, *The Concise Townscape*, Architectural Press (London), 1961.
15. Design Guide Bulletin 32, 'Residential Roads and Footpaths'. The first edition was published in 1977 with the second edition published in October 1998, by the then DETR, adding considerations of security and traffic calming.
16. Paul Grover, 'Introduction', in Hilary French (ed) *Accommodating Change: Innovation in Housing*, Circle 33 and the Architecture Foundation (London), 2002, p 11.
17. Neave Brown, op cit, p 9.

Syntax (www.spacesyntax.com/housing) or a recent Commission for Architecture and the Built Environment (CABE) workshop in Blackburn,[7] has underlined that though routes for traffic combined with continuous perimeter development often prove most effective at reducing crime in residential areas, 'spaces from which you were least likely to be burgled were well integrated linear residential through roads with good numbers of "intervisible" dwellings facing the road on either side with no gaps'.[8]

The car remains the ongoing conundrum of how to design successful communal space. As the fulfilment of the narcissistic tendency – one's own private space even in public – the spatial freedom it provides to consume and transport goods back to that locus of consumption – the home – is balanced against the freedom of kids to play safely outdoors (setting aside the worry of 'stranger danger', exacerbated by the unregarded waste of so much communal space).

The failure of many postwar housing schemes chimed with the political climate created by Margaret Thatcher who, echoing de Tocqueville, summed up the ethos of an era when she stated that 'there's no such thing as society'.[9] The idea of 'home' lost its elasticity, retreating indoors away from any sense of neighbourhood, into the mean 'panic room' of bottom-line developer housing, freed from any Parker Morris space standards[10] and surrounded by the dead space of the gated community.

Conversely, in the wake of the Urban Task Force and following on from the strictures of the Egan Report[11] on quantity and quality of product delivery in the building industry, the present government is supporting a plethora of new initiatives designed to ameliorate the mistakes of the past and tackling that most elusive measurement – quality of life – particularly in relation to public and communal space. Thus one of the stated aims of 'CABE Space', launched at the Urban Summit in October 2002, is 'to seek to influence the creation of new well-managed open space as part of the Housing Market Renewal programme and involve communities more directly in the management of neighbourhood spaces'.[12]

Meanwhile, the 'home zone' initiative – 'a street or group of streets designed primarily to meet the interests of pedestrians and cyclists rather than motorists, opening up the street for social use' – is not a particularly new approach but just a glorified traffic-calming measure where 'benches or play may be introduced' that can turn 'streets into valued public spaces ...

a safer place for children to play ... [and] ... lead to a reduction in street crime'.[13]

On its own, the 'home zone' initiative seems yet another mechanism to domesticate the car as the sole solution to creating successful communal space rather than offering any attempt to manipulate all other aspects of the space itself, and is perhaps rather misguided, potentially further blurring any remaining boundaries in the shared space of residential neighbourhoods. However, when successfully applied as part of a palette of measures, as at Newhall (see opposite), it provides the catalyst for the revival of ideas on space, such as those of Gordon Cullen,[14] and allows enlightened councils like Harlow to interpret more creatively Highway Standards such as DB32.[15]

Integrating and mitigating the presence of the car remains a key factor but this should always be an adjunct to the primary manipulation of the built form and the spaces it creates. Encouragingly, many contemporary schemes are exhibiting innovative new forms of space creation particularly in regard to threshold space, although often based on past typologies.

Last year, Paul Grover wrote of the short-listed entries for 'Accommodating Change', the housing competition run by the Architecture Foundation for Circle 33: 'Whilst the forms might appear familiar, differences appear in the handling of shared spaces, the ability to accommodate functional and occupational change, and a renewed interest in the street and the neighbourhood.'[16]

Peter Barber Architects' winning scheme re-establishes a familiar terrace street pattern yet is formed of interlocking maisonettes each with their own courtyard gardens at ground and first floors. And in schemes ranging from Chorlton Park, Manchester, by Stephenson Bell Architects for Irwell Valley Housing Association to Staiths South Bank, designed by Wayne and Gerardine Hemingway and the Ian Darby Partnership for George Wimpey City, other variations of familiar patterns of perimeter blocks – such as private gardens backed on to naturally protected communal 'home zones', and raised ground floors with narrow but defined transition zones to the street – are being utilised to achieve higher densities and provide innovative models for the future.

Encouragingly, these examples and the three case studies in this article, which range from an inner-urban block to an urban-fringe infill site and a greenfield development, were commissioned by both commercial developers and registered social landlords, underlining how innovation depends not just on designers but also on imaginative client bodies, looking to relearn old lessons: 'The stuff of housing can be seen as the raw material for fashioning a public realm, complex and hierarchical and finally giving "place" to every home.'[17]

Assisted Self-Build Housing, Broadway Estate, Tilbury, Essex, 2002–03

Architect: Sergison Bates Architects
Client: New Islington and Hackney Housing Association
End-user representative: New Essex Housing Association
Number of units: 10
Density: 167 units per hectare

The site itself, lying at the edge of the estate and bounded by the walls of surrounding properties, was an area of dead space where burnt-out cars ended up. The project effectively acts as a plug, enclosing this area to form a semiprivate courtyard (the architects describe this as 'throwing a net around a space') in which a new two-storey apartment building is placed. This contains one- and two-bedroom units with the potential for open-plan living areas that can be adapted or personalised.

Entrance to the units is via a raised boardwalk at ground level and a timber verandah above, providing the principal social spaces of the building, which it is hoped residents will adopt as part of their own space. Ground-floor units also have private backyards.

The scheme, maintained by New Essex Housing Association, represents the first stage of a regeneration programme for the community, providing low-cost rental accommodation for young people.

The construction has involved four of the residents, hopefully providing the kernel to foster a sense of ownership and community in the scheme from the outset.

Inevitably with this type of project, compromises have had to be made, with the verandah only being half as wide as originally intended, thus having more the scale of an access balcony than a space to sit out in. Additionally the budget for external works was cut to a minimum in an essentially simple scheme where the success or failure of the communal courtyard can come down to quality of materials or the detailing of a gate post.

Ultimately, though, the design can only create the potential, not a proscriptive condition, for fostering a sense of ownership, of 'somewhere'. As the architects describe it, the modest ambition for the scheme is that at the very least 'it takes responsibility for a space, giving the opportunity for something to happen but if it doesn't it's not a failure'.

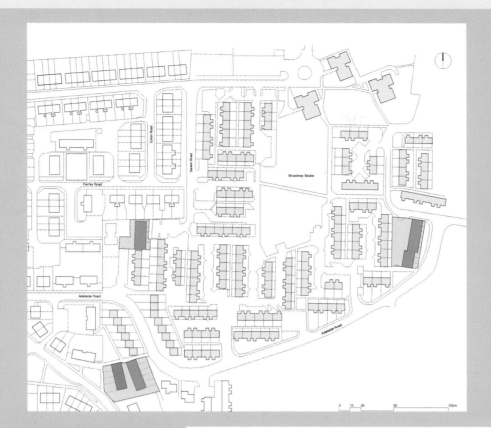

Assisted Self-Build Housing, Broadway Estate, Tilbury, Essex, 2002–03

Opposite top left
Typical existing communal area on the Broadway Estate.

Opposite top right
Semiprefabricated open-panel timber frame under construction.

Opposite, bottom
Perspective of west facade. Externally the building expresses its multi-occupancy through a low-key but highly tuned visual and spatial identity, with the raised boardwalk at ground level and a timber verandah above linking the individual units together.

Top left
Site plan. The scheme (centre left) is essentially an infill located in the run-down and troubled 1960s Broadway Estate, which consists of a series of tower blocks adjacent to a communal landscaped area, and two-storey houses staggered around access roads and pedestrian walkways and alleys. Many of the latter have had to be fenced off as they have become magnets for crime. Two other possible infill sites are also identified here.

Middle and bottom
Plan and section. Internally the scheme seeks to improve upon the 'basic' domestic provisions offered in social housing, including higher-than-standard ceilings, increased daylight provision and flexibility in room layouts. The construction is of a semi-prefabricated open-panel frame, clad in a rain screen of cement panels and larch timber boards and raised slightly from the ground by concrete pads.

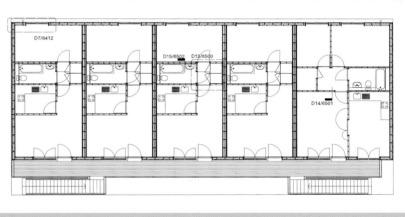

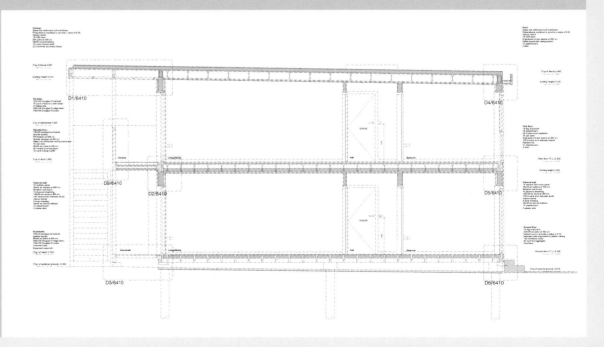

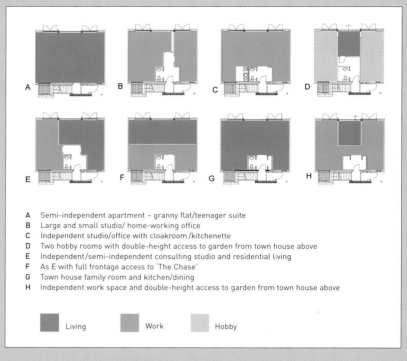

A   Semi-independent apartment – granny flat/teenager suite
B   Large and small studio/ home-working office
C   Independent studio/office with cloakroom /kitchenette
D   Two hobby rooms with double-height access to garden from town house above
E   Independent/semi-independent consulting studio and residential living
F   As E with full frontage access to 'The Chase'
G   Town house family room and kitchen/dining
H   Independent work space and double-height access to garden from town house above

▮ Living   ▮ Work   ▮ Hobby

Newhall, Harlow, Essex, 2001– 04
Architect: Proctor and Matthews Architects
Master planner: Roger Evans Associates
Client: Newhall Projects Ltd
Number of units: 82
Density: 52.6 units per hectare/223 habitable
rooms per hectare

This development, on a greenfield site on the edge of Harlow, is predominantly low rise, its planning intended to reflect 'the higher densities and urban qualities of traditional villages, not those of a contemporary suburban development'.

Consisting of a hierarchy of streets, lanes and mews courts, the emphasis given to the structure of external spaces is designed to encourage community interaction. Additionally there are plans to set up a neighbourhood association, with each household

paying £60 annually towards the upkeep of communal areas, designed to give a sense of shared ownership and control to the residents.

The mews areas are developed as gravelled courts at the heart of perimeter blocks, accessing integral garages but acting as simply articulated 'home zones', naturally surveyed, controlled and programmed by those living around them, where children's play is well supervised and allowing for communal activities such as neighbourhood barbecues.

This layout imaginatively combines the need to increase density with what has proved an aspirational housing 'typology'. The mews flats, all unique in layout with individual front doors and small private external gardens (enabling minimal upkeep), but access to extensive shared communal spaces, have proved very popular.

The palette of materials responds directly to the master-plan design code. A horizontal datum of red-brick garden- and ground-floor walls stitches the streets and external spaces together, creating a regular but continuous perimeter block and forming an urban edge

The architects have described how the creation of thresholds is very important to their designs. Thus at street level, panels of rubble and limestone gabions project to form verandahs, marking and emphasising the entrance to each dwelling, and giving a rhythm to the street. These are combined with a series of louvres and screens, mediating a level of overlooking and being overlooked, and completing a complex animation of the act of entry to each dwelling, providing what the architects describe as 'a framework for interaction'. **Δ**

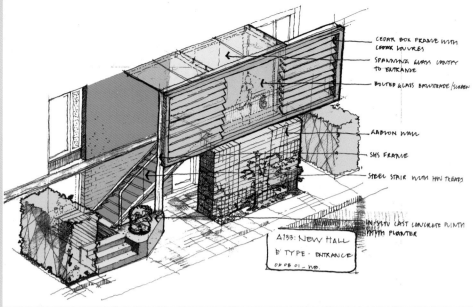

CEDAR BOX FRAME WITH
CEDAR LOUVRES

SPANNING GLASS CANOPY
TO ENTRANCE

BOLTED GLASS BALUSTRADE/SCREEN

GABION WALL

SHS FRAME

STEEL STAIR WITH HW TREADS

IN SITU CAST CONCRETE PLINTH
WITH PLANTER

A133: NEW HALL
'E' TYPE · ENTRANCE
06 08 01 — WB.

**Newhall, Harlow, Essex,
2001–04**

Opposite, top left
Site plan.

Opposite, top right
Typical plans of E-type units.
Layouts of units have been
configured to provide flexible
living accommodation
supporting changing lifestyles
and circumstances, aimed
at a long-term sustainable
community. Thus some
dwellings offer the potential to
have office or studio space at
ground level directly accessing
the street, whilst sliding
walls facilitate the creation
of spaces for a nursery, an
au-pair unit, home working
or a granny flat upstairs.

Opposite bottom and this page,
bottom
Typical street facades.
At ground level a horizontal
datum of red-brick garden-
and ground-floor walls
stitches the streets and
external spaces together
whilst upper levels are of
rough-sawn dark-stained
timber shiplap boards,
traditionally employed in
farm buildings in the area.

This page, top right
Typical entrance elements.
Panels of rubble and limestone
gabions forming verandahs,
combined with a series of
louvres and screens, animate
the threshold to each dwelling.

This page, top left and middle
Two views of the model
of a typical mews court.

The Swedish Home

In the mid-1980s the Swedish government pulled out of housing provision and by the mid-1990s production was almost at a standstill. **Ola Nylander**, the author of *Architecture of the Home*, provides the background to this crisis and looks at how the situation has been kick-started at the beginning of the new millennium, illustrating some architectural models of good practice and discussing how IKEA and Skanska have invested in this area.

Sweden has never built social housing. Quite the opposite. Sweden's ambition for housing construction, established by the governing Social Democratic Party during the 1930s was clear: 'Only the best is good enough for the people.' That all citizens were to have good homes was one of the cornerstones of the Swedish model.

However, Swedish housing construction is in the midst of change as the national housing policy that gave Sweden its international reputation as the land of housing construction with a passion for social justice in the 1940s and 1950s was deconstructed 15 years ago.

During the 1950s, new and aesthetically appealing ideas bore fruit in the form of high-qualitative housing architecture. Architects played an important role in this development and government-organised study and research produced knowledge of the functions and dimensions of the home. By forming municipal housing companies, housing in which profit was not the first objective could be developed, and rental apartments in blocks became the most common way of living in Sweden. The chief purpose of the national housing policy was to meet the acute need for housing that, in the early 1900s, made Sweden a country with nearly the lowest standard of living in Europe, second only to Portugal. By the mid-1970s the situation was the reverse; Sweden was no longer at the bottom of the list, but at the top as having the highest standard of living in Europe.

The flip side of this major investment in housing construction was that quantity came before quality. During the 1960s and 1970s government interference in housing construction grew, and an increasingly meagre residential architecture developed that was adapted to regulations and loans. Far too much traditional architectural knowledge disappeared in rigid government requirements and a one-sided rational relationship to the home and living.

During the two decades between 1965 and 1985, Swedish taxpayers financed housing construction, and by the late 1980s the national housing policy had an annual expenditure of 3 billion euros. By means of steering housing construction, the government could counteract swings in the business cycle; when Swedish exports dropped, housing construction rose and labour could be shifted to the building sector.

Thus many homes were built during the 1960s and 1970s – 100,000 apartments annually, which is quite a lot for a country with a

population of slightly less than 9 million! But during the 1980s production slowed somewhat to between 60,000 and 70,000 apartments annually, and during this period many large and cheap apartments were built that unfortunately were incredibly dismal in terms of architecture.

During the late 1980s, the national housing policy became an increasingly more troublesome expenditure for the country's finances. Government-financed grants for housing construction came under discussion and began to be phased out, being completely withdrawn in the early 1990s when the conservative parties came to power in Sweden. Construction and living began to be taxed and the conditions for housing construction were dramatically changed. Instead of a national expenditure, housing became an annual income of 2–3 billion euros. At the same time, Sweden was hit by a deep recession;

Skanska/IKEA, BoKlok, Helsingborg, southern Sweden, 1999

Left and right
BoKlok is an initiative for low housing costs that comes from construction company Skanska and furniture manufacturer IKEA. The block has guaranteed rents of 450 euros per month for 65 square metres. A rational production in a housing construction factory results in lower production costs. The two companies began by asking what the residents wanted and how much they could pay before building the block.

Kjell Forshed, Västra Kungshall, Karlskrona, Sweden, 1993

Above left
A pronounced attribute of the apartment is the long, angled axis that transverses three rooms, an axis that makes use of the full length of the apartment. Wide openings between them create a distinct chain of rooms – the axis is perceived as stronger.

Above right
The impression of axiality in a home begins the moment we enter one of its points of departure. In the hall, we are met by an angled axis that transverses the full length of the apartment. The axis crosses three rooms and makes maximum use of the apartment's length. The point of departure for the axis is the loggia and the influx of daylight. The target of the axis is the window in the gable wall.

housing construction came to a standstill and in the mid-1990s only slightly more than 10,000 apartments were being built annually.

The new situation caused the players on the building market to reconsider. The John Matsson construction company was the quickest to adapt, choosing to build tenant co-ops in exclusive areas, primarily in major urban centres such as Stockholm, Gothenburg and Malmö. The company also understood the importance of studying the market by interviewing residents about the kinds of homes they sought. JM was a winner among construction companies during the 1990s, while the municipal housing companies experienced major setbacks.

The municipal housing companies had built the majority of the large-scale monotonous residential areas where people no longer wanted to live. Thus municipal production of new housing came to a stop owing to the many empty apartments, and in some small municipalities apartment blocks were even torn down. From totally dominating new housing production in the early 1980s, by 2001 the share of new

construction by municipal housing companies had sunk to a low 17 per cent.

Those who could followed JM's successful formula, and under these circumstances residential architecture gained greater significance. Once the home became marketable goods, good architecture became a way of making the home attractive and easier to sell. The quality of material and detailing, the quality of spatial figures and the organisation of space all rose, and the increasingly more attractive residential architecture created greater public interest in housing planning and interior decoration; a number of periodicals were started, books were written on the subject and there are currently architecture and design programmes with a particular focus on the home on nearly all TV channels.

During the late 1990s the business cycle began to climb again, and more people demanded new housing. The costs of housing grew and tenant co-ops became a lucrative business for construction companies. However, there was no longer a national housing policy that took into account the growing demand. With the new heavy taxes it was still difficult to make rental apartments into a lucrative business. In more recent

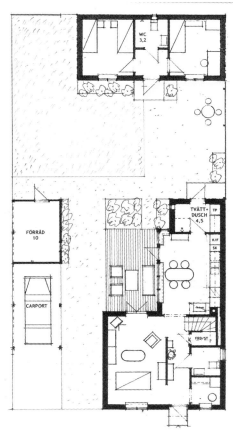

Kjell Forshed, Birgittas Trädgårdar, Vadstena, Sweden, 2002

Above left and right
Outdoors there is openness and contact between home and garden. This represents outdoor space where the family can gather out of view of neighbours or people on the street – an unusual attribute for a rental unit.

Right
Floor plan. The furnishing scheme and garden are based on interviews with residents. The home can be extended with an annex – a courtyard building – that can be used as a room for a teenager, or a guest room, work room or room to let.

Far right, top and bottom
Many beautiful and well-made details, such as the windowsills, window sashes and base moulding, are evidence of good craftsmanship.

Jens Th Arnfred, Kv Nielsen,
Hestra, Borås, Sweden, 1994

Above
Large windows almost dissolve
the border between the
natural landscape and the
home, rounding corners to
create an open and airy home.
Wild grass, heather and
lingonberry sprigs grow only
a few feet from the buildings.
This is the result of an
unusually tactful construction
process – a sign of
conscientiousness.

to live'. The most expensive form of living is in a rental.
In 2000, tenants in rental apartments spent 26 per cent
of their income on rent, compared with a cost of 20 per
cent for those who owned their homes. The average
cost for a newly built apartment in 2001 was slightly
more than 100 euros per square metre per year.

In 2001 a small government-financed investment
grant was created to increase housing construction.
The grant entitled purchasers to 12,000 euros per
apartment. This year an additional grant has been
created whereby companies that build small
apartments (a maximum of 60 square metres) will
receive a tax relief that lowers VAT from the current 25
per cent to 6 per cent. Nevertheless, problems remain.
Still too little housing is being built and it is difficult
to find housing in Stockholm, Gothenburg and Malmö,
while at the same time there are plenty of empty
apartments in small towns. In 2001 there were 45,000
vacant apartments in Sweden.

Production costs for housing construction vary
greatly. An extreme example is the HSB housing tower
in Malmö, designed by Calatrava. Though the tower is
40 storeys high, it is a landmark scheme with a twisted
form, with production costs at 4,000 euros per square
metre; in smaller towns with cheaper land, apartment
blocks are being built for 1,300 euros per square metre.

Paradoxically, one of the few initiatives for low
housing costs comes from two large private companies,
construction company Skanska and furniture
manufacturer IKEA. The two companies have launched
their BoKlok (Live Wisely) block with a rent of 450-500
euros per month for a one-bedroom apartment of 52
square metres. BoKlok is a simple modular construction
built in two storeys. Rational production in a housing
construction factory results in lower construction costs;
though the BoKlok block has different facades and
colours, the content remains the same wherever it is
built. The block is interesting from many different
perspectives, primarily because it is
not an experiment in living and the home. Instead, the
builders ask what the residents want and how much they
can pay, and then build such a block. Simple! The block
includes amenities, for example, hedges, gates,
flagpoles and cherry trees, taken directly from housing
surveys in which tenants have expressed what they
desire. In Sweden tenants can order apartments at IKEA
stores, and so far 1,200 BoKlok apartments have been
built in Sweden, Norway and Finland, where they are
very popular. There are also plans to launch this concept
in Denmark in 2004.The period of change in housing has,
thus far, not given any clear indication of new directions
or trends in Swedish residential architecture. Many
homes inspired by Functionalism are still being designed
despite the public desire for richness of perception and
inspiration. However, two architects in particular, in an
interesting way and from different approaches,

years, new housing production has increased
and in 2001 slightly more than 15,000
apartments were built. The forecast for 2003
is 20,000 apartments. Currently Sweden has
a record low interest rate of roughly 5 per cent.

For the Social Democratic Party, which has
been back in power for a number of years,
housing policy is a dilemma. It knows that the
former policy with generous government grants
did not work particularly well and was very costly.
At the same time the government is criticised
because the housing that is being built is too
expensive for ordinary people to afford. In 2001
production costs per square metre for apartments
in blocks was 2,000 euros. Construction costs
increase by 10 per cent per year.

For the above reason, many people want
new government-financed grants for housing
construction, 'so that ordinary people can afford

Jens Th Arnfred, Tre Gudor, Viken, Sweden, 2002

Above
The buildings stand close to the street in the same manner as older buildings in the fishing community in Viken. Facing the courtyard, the buildings open up with large glazed sections and private yards. The buildings are clad in corrugated black fibre-reinforced cement sheeting with elements of white-washed light brick sections. The interiors of the buildings are in dramatic contrast to the dark exteriors.

have successfully developed the qualitative, nonmeasurable attributes of residential architecture. Kjell Forshed and the Dane, Jens Th Arnfred, have both been, and are still, vital to the development of the Swedish home.

Kjell Forshed of Brunnberg & Forshed Arkitektkontor is a leading residential architect in Sweden. Forshed was active in developing ideas of close low-rise housing in the 1970s, and in 1993 designed the residential area Västra Kungshall, for the Bo93 housing expo, in the little coastal town of Karlskrona. His design paved the way for greater awareness of the importance of the quality of materials and care in detailing, as well as the importance of daylight and axiality.

The purchaser was the National Federation of Tenants' Savings and Building Societies (HSB), which since the 1920s has been building and owns housing throughout the country. The floor plan of 82 square metres was based on six squares with a chain of rooms and the potential for a circular loop through these. The pine floorboards, steeped in lye to lighten them, are an example of the strong impression that

can be created with materials. The pine floor combined with well-planned and aesthetically pleasing detailing gives the occupants the feeling that someone cares. Residents are met by an architecture that has dignity, and materials and detailing that signal: 'I matter to someone else.' Deep splayed sides of the window niches, distinct corners and marked spatial contours enhance the room's enclosure. The glassed-in balcony – the loggia – with its open space is a clear contrast to the room's enclosure.

The measurements of the rooms allow for flexibility, which differs from Modernism's functional differentiation in which each room is designed for a specific purpose. And this generality gives the home a unique breadth of interpretation in which the residents can determine the use of space and the degree to which it is public or private.

Forshed has returned to this architecture, sated with architectural values, in his subsequent commissions. One residential project that was completed in 2002 is Birgittas Trädgårdar in Vadstena, one of Sweden's oldest towns. The project is minor, only eight units, and the purchaser is the municipal housing company Vadstena Fastighets AB. The floor area of each two-bedroom apartment is 90 square

Jens Th Arnfred, Tre Gudor, Viken, Sweden, 2002

Above
Bay windows on the upper floor effectively function as illuminating lanterns. Deep window sashes fill with daylight. Daylight enriches movement from the large room – the living room – to the smaller room – the bedroom. An extra attribute is the slope of the ceiling, which follows the slope of the roof and creates greater volume.

metres, and the outer walls are prefabricated. The project was built by small local companies, resulting in apartments with unique qualities for rent at reasonable prices; the production cost for the project was slightly more than 2,000 euros per square metre, which gives a rent of SEK1,100 per square metre per year.

At Birgittas Trädgårdar, the attributes of the rental unit have been further developed. The project is marked by an aggressive investment in quality. Instead of building cheap rental units for those who cannot afford to buy their own apartments or houses, Birgittas Trädgårdar offers rental units at ground level where the residents have four walls of their own and a private, little, protected garden. A courtyard building – an annex – can be added to each apartment, which means a family can remain in the apartment even if the size of the family increases. The heart of the apartment is the beautiful roomy kitchen, which is the lightest and most open space. The kitchen is also the

natural target for the axiality and movement of the floor plan. Thus the housing in Birgittas Trädgårdar unites the untroubled and comfortable living of rental apartments with high architectonic quality.

In 1993, Jens Th Arnfred, who in many projects has developed openness and transparency in residential architecture, was awarded the Kasper Sahlin Prize (a major Swedish architecture prize) for Kv Nielsen, a residential project in Borås, a town in central Sweden. Kv Nielsen offers simple homes, rental units, built by municipal housing company AB Bostäder i Borås. Narrow black buildings radiate from two hillocks covered with oak trees. An open space between floors, together with a two-storey window, gives each apartment an open character that interacts with the surrounding natural landscape, which has been preserved through tactful construction. Located just a few metres outside the glass openings there are meadows, big trees and large, moss-covered rocks. Conscientious attention to detail creates a feeling of thoughtfulness. The location's history is intact and is vital to the resident's comfort and sense of home.

In the spring of 2002, Jens Arnfred's most recent residential project, Tre Gudor, was completed – some 40 apartments located on the edge of the centre of the tiny community of Viken in southern Sweden. The purchaser was HSB. Many of the attributes from the Kv Nielsen housing project can also be found here, though Tre Gudor also represents a renaissance for distinct street space. The housing, coupled with utility buildings and carports, creates enclosed and aesthetically appealing urban space.

The housing in Tre Gudor is close together and low rise with rich interaction between indoors and outdoors. And there is a stringency in the detailing and choice of materials that is found far too seldom in Swedish housing production.

All of the projects described here explore new directions for the Swedish home – simple and aesthetic housing in which good architecture has been obtained at a reasonable production cost. These are attractive homes with good economy from a long-term perspective. These are apartments that encourage a wealth of varied impressions – designed by architects who have realised the significance of architecture for residents and the home.

It is gratifying that Swedish residential architecture is once again approaching the high quality of that of the 1940s and 1950s. Yet a final stringency and crystal-clear objective is still missing. We have a way to go, but we are on the right path. ⌂

Ola Nylander, *Architecture of the Home*, John Wiley & Sons, 2002 (ISBN 0-470-8787-5), PB £19.99/US$40.00, is available from all good architectural book shops and direct from Wiley at www.wileyeurope.com or in the US from www.wiley.com

EMERGENCY DWELLING

Mark Prizeman explains the current state of emergency housing provision, in which Western countries commonly provide unsuitable prefabricated shelters in an insensitive and economically self-serving manner. Looking at particular examples, such as the 1999 earthquake in Turkey, the war in the Balkans and the 1996 earthquake in Kobe, Japan, he suggests means of rectifying the situation so that the inherent building intelligence within a culture is put to use, and tools and techniques, rather than inflexible solutions, are supplied.

With around 20 million people worldwide currently being sheltered by the United Nations High Commission for Refugees (UNHCR) the issue of designing emergency shelters that are suitable for a range of climates and situations becomes ever more urgent. The possibilities for the design of these shelters are irresistible to many a designer, combining the issues of modern technology, social righteousness, prefabrication, mobility and the allure of being 'temporary'. Thus over the years huge numbers of designs have been presented to non-governmental organisations (NGOS), promising rational solutions to messy problems, using the perceived power of technology and sympathy to provide for the needy by transferring knowledge through the product.

A brief perusal of a patent library will bring to light many well-intentioned but ultimately deeply unsuitable inventions for the provision of shelter for victims of disaster. Disasters are seen as impending events and the ingenuity of being able to solve an imagined state of crisis, be it an earthquake or the threat of nuclear warfare, produces many examples such as the illustrated patent for a 'fallout shelter' tent below.

Herein lies part of the problem: the patent is the method by which an idea is registered, before it becomes a commodity as the commercial intellectual property usually of a particular manufacturer. It will be from the manufacturer's factory, at a time dependent on the factory's production capacity, that the design will be dispatched, the design perhaps being totally inappropriate to the culture and climate of the disaster. As a reaction following arguments with manufacturers, Buckminster Fuller, designer of the ill-fated prefabricated Dymaxion House, never patented his later ideas, so that they could be free for all to use.

Fred Cuny, the late post-disaster shelter relief authority, wrote in 1978: 'Let me emphasise this fact: new housing types are not needed. Every relief agency has a file cabinet full of bright ideas submitted by graduate students, industrial designers and architects, which offer the ultimate solution to the world's housing problems. Thousands of designs and concepts have been drawn, some have been developed and even a few have made it to the field.'[1]

Designing innovative shelters for the variety of disaster scenarios encountered and the affected societies requires a certain specialisation in both climate and sociology; for example, winter in eastern Anatolia in Turkey is very different to summer in central Africa.

Emergency housing is the classic example of how top-down paternalistic aid and planning uses exported 'ideal' Western values of lifestyle to enforce allegiance, ultimately acting as a self-serving, efficient set of solutions for the donor. Here, economic benefit is gained by the industries of donor countries and not the victim state's manufacturers. Aid agencies compete for allocations of programmes in 'aid

Previous page
Tunnel tents being used for families from rental accommodation with charity donations on display. Golçuk, Turkey, 1999

Right
Patent for a tent to be erected in the run-up to nuclear war and to be inhabited until fallout has reached acceptable levels.

Far right
Screen print by Mungo McCosh sold in aid of relief for the 1999 Turkish earthquake (deprem) survivors, illustrating the makeshift shelters made by the communities.

Opposite, top
Improvised shelter in central Golçuk, 1999, adjacent to a crack caused by the foreshore slipping.

Opposite, bottom
Cotton bell tents supplied by the Red Crescent, housing single men from rented accommodation. Golçuk, Turkey, 1999.

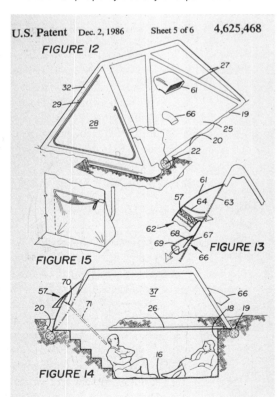

auctions', which cynically are often seen as serving only to further the public profile of the aid agency and thus its cash flow.

There is no example of the provision of relief shelters, beyond tents, from one nation to another prior to the Second World War. The political manipulations that were possible in such provision included the settlement of nomadic societies and denials of land reform, which have now only exacerbated the problem. External aid adds another potential cost in the cultural redirection of the affected society. Today, some countries refuse any external aid as it always carries a price – for example, conceding the right to the donor country to build a military base.

It is not only the agendas of the providers but also the types of shelter they provide that are questionable. And, often culturally unacceptable, physically useless or badly sited, they often arrive late. For example, the Oxfam prefabricated shelter provision for the 1976 earthquake in a remote rural area of Turkey arrived four weeks after the government's permanent replacement housing had been completed.

The potential scale of disasters is also now increasing. Large dislocations following politico/ethnic conflicts and economic migrations, along with the rapid urbanisation in the last quarter-century of areas prone to natural disasters, have made the problem worse.

Earthquakes now occur directly beneath large modern cities with sprawling high-density urban expansions. Climate change exposes fresh possibilities for the rapid destruction of the natural habitat from flooding and storms, and wars rumble on. The two locations that victims find themselves in are either almost amongst their failed dwellings or in an alien land already inhabited by others.

Thus the preconceptions of designing and manufacturing rapidly deployable replacement shelters need to be readdressed. What can be provided falls into two categories: complete dwellings such as tents and the more permanent cabin or the deployment of materials for self-build. Another opportunity is the provision of services that can accelerate self-help recovery and restore a community's ability to 'bounce back'. The ability of a design to be rapidly deployed and the local economic and environmental consequences of such an action are paramount to its success.

The bodies that pay for the designs are either governments or aid agencies. The ultimate aims and the specialisation of provision will vary from agency to agency and class of victim. However, the need for their being temporary remains important as the designs must fit into a larger picture of reconstruction.

The tent, the most effectively deployable form of prefabricated dwelling, is also the most favoured as it is truly temporary. Tents can be stored and transported easily since they are usually designed for that great industrial nomad – the army. Though the many new designs use aluminium or plastic frames and new fabrics, they don't as yet provide all the requirements for the sustenance of family life, particularly in changeable climates where there are the problems of insulating against a cold wind or ventilating a sun-baked shelter.

More rigid shelters, such as plywood-, hardboard- or even cardboard-panelled constructions, by their very bulk arrive upwards of a fortnight after the disaster to settle select victims on a more comfortable basis. Although they are considered temporary they are inevitably permanent additions to the environment, occupied or not, and provide a higher degree of security, particularly for families and women. And though they are inherently culturally unsuitable – many relief villages have remained empty for years due to bad siting and misunderstanding the needs of particular communities – they can create a secure foothold for disaster victims.

Victims sometimes have no choice and are forced to take whatever the government or aid agency gives them. For example, in the 2001 Guatemala earthquake, lightweight corrugated tin and timber housing units were rapidly erected by voluntary organisations and the army to settle the scores of urban shanty dwellers left homeless. These were occupied despite the fact that they reached 65°C during the day and were nicknamed 'microwaves'.

The accepted theory is that in order to facilitate

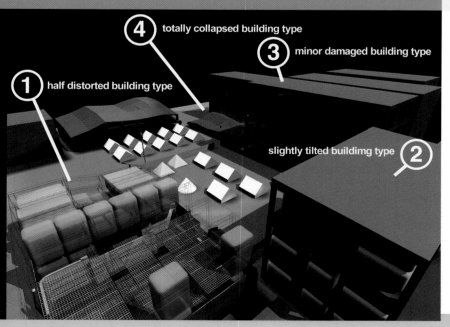

① half distorted building type
④ totally collapsed building type
③ minor damaged building type
② slightly tilted buildimg type

recovery the minimum required for immediate shelter should be provided, and preferably from a local source for the purpose of encouraging self-reliance and thus regenerating economic activity. This avoids carting unsuitable and unnecessary prefabricated artefacts halfway round the globe. It can be assumed that local labour will be cheap and materials expensive. This, ironically, is the converse of the industrial situation in the prefabrication business. Most people, when on their home ground, would prefer the money that is used to transport the prefabricated units to be used to help them rebuild their own homes and industries, which tends to be faster anyway.

Many of the problems of, and opportunities for, shelter design can be identified in the case study of the 17 August 1999 earthquake near Istanbul, Turkey. The Anatolian fault line that runs across northern Turkey behaves in much the same way as the San Andreas fault beneath San Francisco. It also runs beneath large recent conurbations where the threat is well understood.

Golçuk, Yalova and the other towns along the southern shore of the Marmara sea are resorts and holiday towns. The inhabitants are, in the main, the middle class or retired who invested what seemed to be a small price for a seaside apartment. But these new five-storey concrete-slab buildings are often constructed using smooth reinforcement bars that have no bond with the concrete they are supposedly reinforcing. In the event of an earthquake, these pancake down into one-storey-high stacks of fractured slab, or topple over. The extent of the damage and the spiralling death toll during the 1999 earthquake seemed to numb the government, and initial attempts at rescue and relief were criticised. The truth is more probably that the extensive rupturing of the physical communication infrastructure and the scale of the devastation meant that it was impossible to manoeuvre resources into the swathe of destruction that was being electronically reported.

The population was resettled and divided according to property status. The apartment owners were encamped in UN barrel tents complete with their own leisure facilities and internal camp currency. The hostel dwellers were housed in cotton bell tents provided by the Red Crescent, and those in between were housed in varying degrees of comfort and military orderliness, with traditional felt-covered yurts provided by the Mongolian government proving particularly popular.

Three or four weeks later the more permanent 'temporary' shelter-types were being delivered from local factories – prefabricated, insulated aluminium 'sheds' with two serviced rooms in each, designed to house two family units (provided they had children and relinquished the rights to their former homes). Divisions between sleeping, cooking and living took the form of fabric internal dividers, and furniture such as beds was issued to make up the shortfall in salvaged furniture. Sited in large camps on virgin hillsides outside the towns, these constructed communities were expected to occupy the dwellings for a minimum of two years until it would be possible to permanently rehouse them.

However, the environmental damage caused by bulldozing the land for the foundation slabs is irreversible, for the reason that these virtual shanties will in all probability remain in occupation, if not by the original victims then by the rapidly expanding urban population. (The population of Istanbul grew by a million a year during the 1990s.)

More than 18,000 were killed in the 1999 quakes with 49,000 injured. Over 200,000 were housed in around 130 tented camps and prefabricated cities. By November, a total of 10,960 prefabricated houses had been built with half in occupation. It was anticipated that the entire tented community would be rehoused in the prefabricated units by the end of the year.

Eight months later a large proportion of families was still living in self-made plastic and nylon dwellings in makeshift yet community-bound encampments. Suffering devastating accidental fires caused by unsuitable cooking apparatus, they carry on waiting for the replacement five-storey dwellings that meanwhile are being built with no apparent

difference in construction from those destroyed.

This is not meant as any explicit criticism of the admirable efforts at rescue and recovery work carried out by the Turkish government and aid agencies. It is more a pointer to the direction the responses to events such as this may need to take in the future. It is only by acknowledging the inherent building intelligence within a culture that it is possible to satisfy the demand for shelter. If only this sense could be developed, with a sustainable approach, within the omnipresence of the industrially prefabricated dwelling.

The war in the Balkans forced the resettlement of a number of disparate cultures, and theories as to how to tread the thin line between creating overreliant or underserved refugee encampments were tested to the full. Scenarios ranged from complete welfare provision, from which evolved an overreliant and immovable community, to situations encouraging self-reliance. Competitions for ideas for emergency shelter provision, contemplating how to help alien cultures suffering deprivation, suggested solutions of 'beauty' against practicality. Being provided with a clever adaptable consumer item – a piece of furniture – does not enable someone to rebuild their life. If that person in their former existence had been of any substance these vacuous gestures are futile, patronising misunderstandings of the situation. In fact, tools and techniques are what are

Opposite, top
Golçuk, Turkey, 1999. Open spaces in towns were filled with makeshift shelters for the human survivors and whatever personal belongings could be salvaged. These camp sites were swelled by those fearful of further aftershocks who chose to sleep outside rather than in their homes.

Opposite, middle
Duzçe, Turkey, 1999. Some inhabitants, desirous of remaining near their former homes, places of employment or family, remained in their makeshift improvised shelters whilst the aid programmes distributing emergency shelters for the survivors were put in place.

Opposite, bottom
A project by Architectural Association student Takuya Onishi for stabilising partially damaged structures using air bags and then injecting concrete. This creates new forms of living space but maintains the community and helps the relief. The project strangely foreshadows a Turkish outfit called Seismik Retrovit who sell their system to fearful homeowners from a concrete mixer, offering to inject potentially unstable structures with extra concrete.

Right
Golçuk, Turkey, 1999. Community centre for single men and families from rental accommodation. Notice the land being cleared for an extension to the camp.

needed to rebuild – not solutions. Lateral thinking about the destiny of available resources and their own situation, a skill victims rediscover with amazing speed, will only be helped by the provision of aid that facilitates self-determinism.

With the provision of appropriate basic materials, components and instructions, suitable shelters can be built using people's incredible nascent ability to improvise, and will also provide employment and diversion. Sensible choice, and provision, of materials is essential. Exemplary designs include those provided by the Saath organisation following the earthquake in Gujarat, India, whereby victims could choose from one of five dwelling types, each using a different technique of construction, with each dwelling then manufactured at a newly set up local plant, working prefabrication into the local economy.

Advances in tent design and fabric engineering, when included in self-built tent projects that build on the insights of the now-vanishing nomad designs for fabric shelters – such as the 'black tent', yurt or teepee –can solve the social problems of the army tent. Domes and fabric tunnel tents are marketed widely. They use different tensioning systems facilitated by new flexible materials and appear in different forms in the field. A new British Army tent designed at Dundee University uses a fabric web as its structural arch, achieving a lighter structure than its framed predecessors. And innovative and adaptive components, such as the fabric-fixing Grip Clips made by Shelter Systems, can hold and attach fabric without perforating it. Following their expiry as useful emergency housing, all components should be capable of reuse or ecological disposal.

Understanding exposure to the weather allows the correct dispersal of materials – for example, using woven fabrics in Africa rather than plastic sheets, or gabions rather than fabric – and this needs to be combined with research into new combinations of fabrics that, for instance, when filled provide noise and heat insulation. Local materials can then replace the difficult-to-deploy rigid insulation slabs that in some cases come with the environmentally dubious claim of having a 500-year life span. And there are ideas such as the safer cooking method of the 'solar oven' which uses sunlight to cook rather than fuel.

The 1996 earthquake in the city of Kobe, Japan, was the first to occur beneath a modern metropolis with earthquake-resistant multistorey constructions and transport infrastructures. Natural disasters illustrate the element of human involvement in exacerbating the scale of death and destruction. Different sections of society received different levels

of relief. Working with the lowest paid members of society, the architect Shigura Ban presented at first hand to these workers the designs of his cardboard-tube-and-drinks-crate constructions. By involving the workers in the construction process he was able to make a cost-effective and ecologically acceptable contribution to the problem. However, what is less clear is whether the machines for making these tubes can be used for other materials, and whether the layout, akin to a military camp denying a sense of street, was part of some political imperative.

Displaced communities need guidelines on how to create an urban form that will provide the opportunity for the right mix of services to facilitate regeneration. In Nicaragua, following the 1976 earthquake, Fred Cuny arranged 12 or so single-family-sized tents around communal courtyards, with shared cooking and washing facilities. This lateral piece of thinking produced a remarkable drop in the number of cases of theft and rape, and eased the general tension. The camp also cost 40 per cent less to run than its conventional gridded cousins, and generated cottage industries that eased the process of recovery. In a refugee camp, on the other hand, the general prerogative is on encouraging the victim to return home, therefore nothing is made too comfortable or permanent. Coaxing disaster victims away from reliance, yet providing a secure haven for the victims and their possessions, is a common design dilemma for aid agencies.

The legacy of prefabrication for relief in Britain originated in the government programme instigated in 1942 in response to the impending need for replacement dwellings on the cessation of the Second World War. Questionnaires were prepared and prototypes built. The resulting houses were popular and outlived their intended 10-year design life span – some by as much as 40 years. This period of research and the opportunity to divert an already active local industrial base from one product to another, often using skills inherent to the factory, was unique in that though it was an acceptable solution it was only applicable in that particular situation.

So how can the marriage of industry, designer and user be consummated, without the agency of engagement on site, to develop a vernacular self-build that uses the application of lateral thinking to foster new and appropriate solutions? The benefits of actually asking people what they want and then teaching them effective practice are enormous.

As the Christian Aid newspaper advertising campaign from the 1970s claimed: 'Buy a man a fish and you feed him for a day – Train him how to fish and you feed him for life'. ∆

Note
1. Quoted by Colin Davidson, Université de Montréal, I-Rec Conference on Post-Disaster Shelter, 23 May 2002.

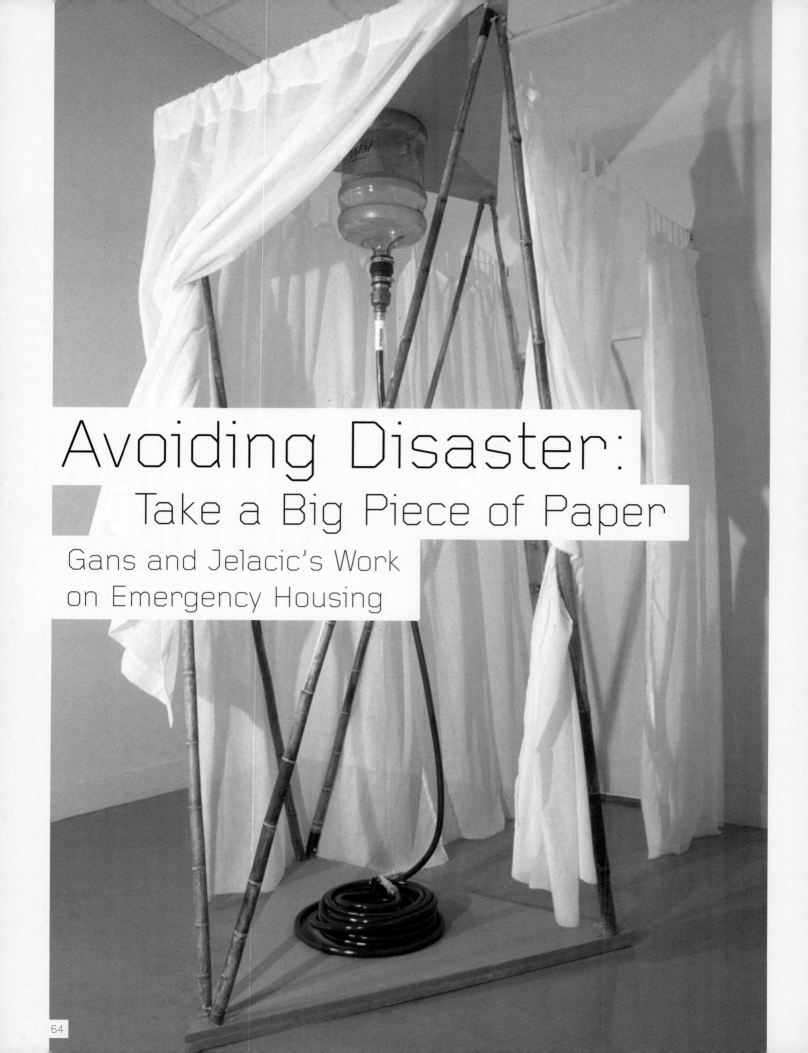

Avoiding Disaster:
Take a Big Piece of Paper

Gans and Jelacic's Work
on Emergency Housing

For the last four years **Deborah Gans** and **Matthew Jelacic** of New York practice Gans & Jelacic have been researching and developing new forms of disaster relief housing. Informed by their research trips to Bosnia and a research stay at the International Centre for Refugees Studies at Oxford University, their work has shifted emergency housing away from ideal forms towards adaptive prototypes that are able to situate themselves in relation to any found situation and the occupant's recurring desires.

praxis' or 'art and politics', is so complete that we neither remember nor imagine an architecture that attempts to intervene.

While disaster relief might seem a speciality item remote from the 'unfinished project of modernity' with its experiments in housing and production, it is required by the one out of every 300 people on earth who face some form of displacement. Displaced persons are previously settled ones who bring with them expectations, desires and values of living, and attempt to enact these in ways that often address not only their extreme situation but also emerging conditions that will eventually face us all. To predicate this flow between the extreme and the normative, consider Le Corbusier's Maison Dom-ino, conceived as a quickly realisable housing system for war-torn Belgium, an awkward and never fully synthesised system of precast concrete columns combined with poured-in-place slabs, which was never built as drawn

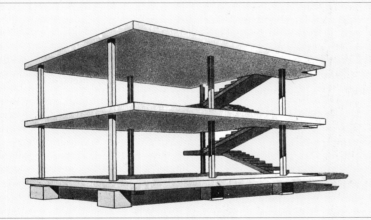

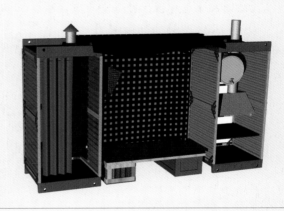

We began working on emergency housing in 1999 in response to an international design competition regarding disaster relief for Kosovo. We chose to enter the competition because it meshed with a larger project of our practice, which is to reimagine terms for the social engagement of architecture. The oddity of such a project to the current mindset is clear from people's fascination with it. We are often interviewed or invited to lecture on our 'altruistic' or 'charitable' work and then asked, often repeatedly, as if no answer quite satisfies: 'Why do you do this?' To us the question reveals the extent to which the world at large considers architecture to be the *Zeitgeist* representation of social issues defined elsewhere. Architecture can monumentalise our pain – but it can't do much about it. The current retreat from architecture as a social art to a cultural one, with art couched in old-fashioned Hegelian terms unmitigated by more current discussions of 'autonomy and

and never deployed for the displaced persons for whom it was intended, and yet became nothing less than the ideogram for modernity.

It was, in fact, not the extreme conditions internal to the camp but the more generalised problems of urban recuperation that drove our thinking in the competition for disaster relief housing for Kosovo. The competition called for an alternative to the tent to be erected within 48 hours from an absolute minimum of materials and to remain in place for as long as two years. The duration of stay made it clear to us that the object would be situated in conditions of infrastructure and environment beyond its power to control. In the larger context of these planning issues, the question became the site rather than the object. Why not recuperate sites of return rather than create better sites of dislocation? Why not develop a physical device that could reconstitute an urban fabric without the support of a civic scale of infrastructure, and that could, as an auxiliary consequence, retool a refugee camp as if it were a city.

Above left
Civic buildings remain in ruins in Bosnia, as photographed on a field trip in 2002.

Above right
House destroyed by scavenging in Bosnia. As in the war in Iraq, looting was part of the process of dismantling and destruction.

Our original proposal was a condensed infrastructure of a privy and a kitchen with hearth/heat source and integral cistern/shower housed in demountable yet load-bearing enclosures. Placed at a distance from one another, the two boxes framed a habitable space in between, wide enough to accommodate a bed. Initially protected with tarps, the distance could subsequently be framed with beams as scaffolding for the construction of the house around it, so that the boxes became a structural and functional core.

Subsequent to the competition we have used additional funding to make site visits to the end users and relief providers, and these have largely confirmed our assumptions. The landscape of Bosnia is, for better or worse, the way we predicted. People want to return home and reproduce their lives, which they are able to do not on the level of monumental infrastructure but on the level of the quotidian units that our project envisions. Apartment houses and civic buildings remain in ruins, but houses and shops have been rebuilt. The nature of the destruction lends itself to this small-scale reconstruction because it often occurs as a conscious dismantling of buildings by their components, like windows and even bricks. Those who flee take them along, and those who return bring them back or scavenge them from the abandoned stock. Thus there is a continuing

supply of recycled local material and prefabricated components that can be used in relation to new structural armatures and cores.

In conditions of mass flight, where long-term displacement and resettlement aren't cushioned by the pre-existing built landscape, nothing is cheaper or more flexible than the tent, that Esperanto sign of disaster relief. However, the justification for more elaborate and costly alternatives does exist in the context of strategic planning, and in the environmental devastation that will occur without it. Refugee camps can be the size of small cities with physical impacts at the environmental and bioregional level so profound that the United Nations High Commission on Refugees (UNHCR) describes them as 'eco-disasters'. The problems include deforestation as refugees collect fuel and building material, consequent soil erosion and loss of biodiversity, water depletion, soil and water contamination from waste, air pollution from cooking fires, and the production of vast amounts of garbage including shipping and construction materials. A successful camp is now measured by its sustainability, thus anticipating our emerging criteria for all cities. Any housing that reduces resource consumption or waste, through physical devices like solar stoves or social devices like cluster kitchens, is worth it.

A most stunning example of the flow from the disastrous to the sustainable, and from the extreme to the everyday, are the three refugee camps of Dadaab, Kenya (total population of 106,000), which moved from initial deforestation and profound disruption of the extant nomadic pastoralism, to an eventual urbanisation of the region on the basis of sustainable herding and a powerful market economy of goods and produce. The camp economy attracts regional traders who stay in the camp hotels, and new settlers who have built quasi-suburbs at its periphery. While such refugee settlements are virtual rather than fully empowered cities in the disenfranchisement of their residents, a blur has occurred at Dadaab to the degree that a call for refugee taxation on the camps' lucrative trade was defeated on the basis of the absence of refugee representation, bringing public debate to the fulcrum point between camp and community. We would bet that just as the colonial cantonments of India in the 19th century became the basis for the Indian 20th-century metropolis, the forced displacement of internal Yoruba wars of the 1830s created the city of Ida ban, and the Congo crisis of independence created Mbuji-Mbayi, the refugee camps of Dadaab describe an urbanism of tomorrow.[2]

Our development of the form of the relief housing continues within our increased understanding of these competing demands of cultural specificity, universal deployment, ecology and production that are its conditions or praxis. For example, the material palette of the housing must consider the attraction of the vernacular and the at-hand, the need to preserve natural resources, the problematic value of raw material more valuable as resale scrap than as housing, and the cost of durability sufficient for the end-game goal of a structure suitable for reuse on the sites of return. Our current proposal is a hybrid of the found, such as cardboard and bamboo, and the imported, such as a high-performance ceramic sheathing.

The conditions of this project force the reconsideration of universal deployment away from the ideal form and towards an ability to situate itself – like an act of simultaneous translation – in relation to recurring desires. We found the most common desire to be the right of return, but second was the desire for TV (not a kitchen or additional square footage), which led to our use of a photovoltaic hook-up. The dominant population of displacement is women, accompanied by children and elderly dependants, who need to assemble and erect the houses without assistance, and this led to our move away from our initial kit of parts towards a folding structure.

A truly lightweight folding structure uses its final geometric configuration for its stability, so that during erection it tends to be unwieldy. Concern with the stability of the structure, especially in unpredictable topographic and soil conditions, led us to shift from a square to triangular form. The risk to women and their dependants when they leave the immediate camp site confirmed the need for an at-hand source of water and fuel for bathing and cooking, but the variation in bathing and cooking

Below
Three forms for relief housing in three materials. Gans & Jelacic's current proposal is a hybrid of the found (cardboard and bamboo) and the imported (high-performance sheathing).

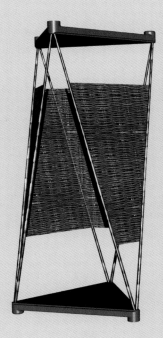

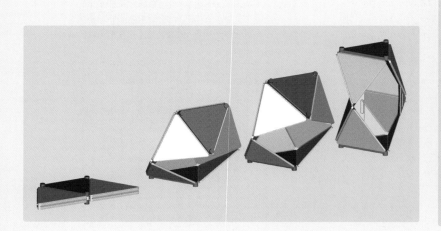

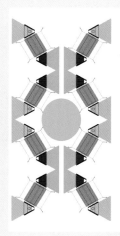

Top left
Unfolding structure by Gans & Jelacic. The need to erect and assemble houses with ease is paramount, as the majority of occupants are women and their dependants.

Top right
Two of Gans & Jelacic's units assembled.

Bottom left
Drawing of possible collective plans of units.

Bottom right
Paired models exhibited at the Slought Network Gallery in Philadelphia.

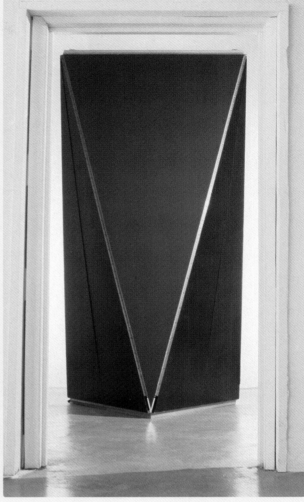

Notes
The title is the first line
of a refugee camp-planning
manual issued in French
by Medecins Sans Frontières.
An excellent article on Dadaab
as a proto-urbanism
is Marc-Antoine Perouse de
Montclos and Peter Mwangi
Kagwani, 'Refugee camps
or cities: the socio-economic
dynamics of Dadaab and
Kakuma camps in Northern
Kenya', *Journal of Refugee
Studies*, vol 13, no 2, pp
205–22.

Above left
Rear view of kitchen unit.

Above right
Front view of kitchen unit.

habits required that these facilities be provided with great flexibility so that, for example, the kitchen can face the privy or the garden or not, or cooking can occur communally or not.

For a recent exhibit at the Slought Network Gallery in Philadelphia we built some full-size models of possible units, where their presence in the context of art has proven contentious, foregrounding the confusion surrounding architecture's autonomy and praxis. Viewed as sculptures (not even with the leeway of installation art) some deemed them unoriginal – finding their geometries known and their presence already established within the framework of minimal art. From our point of view, their originality as well as the cultural specificity of the form is largely irrelevant given the unpredictability of the end game, which is to be embedded deep within a permanent house, determined largely by the inhabitant. While they allow the renewed operation of a site, they are themselves incomplete and dependent on their host city as a form of economy. Incompleteness is a fundamental aspect not of our forms but

for the architecture, which can be fully described only as part of its larger landscape or urban plan, and in its return to its social practice.

The current manuals for planning a refugee camp, besides being terribly basic and cursory in most regards, set out architecture and planning as a subset of health and safety issues, many chapters after the handling of excreta and water and with little thought to their integration or to their long-term consequences. The urbanisation of the world through displaced populations isolated in camps and swelling our existing cities goes on unstrategised, despite the incipient rumbling of ecological guidelines issued by UNHCR.

While the world might be littered with ingenious proposals for emergency shelter, the mining of the complexities of displacement and its impact on our physical and social environments has hardly begun. The first instruction of the manual issued by Doctors Without Borders, 'Take a big sheet of paper', is not as naive as it first sounds but rather the perfect statement of the architect's situation – ever suspended in the tensions between form-giving and the conditions that engender it and to which it must return. In the context of the Dadaabs and the Kosovos we add – just make sure it's big enough. ⚙

Fine Tuning:

How the New York City Housing Authority Makes Housing Work

In a country with a strong anti-urban bias, where owner-occupied single-family houses are the norm, government-owned subsidised housing – especially modern high-rise housing – has always carried a stigma. Except in New York City, where even the wealthy live in apartment towers, a seemingly permanent housing shortage makes public housing attractive to a wide spectrum of people. And, now, an enlightened and imaginative building programme at the New York City Housing Authority is bringing security, recreation and exciting design to 'the projects'. Jayne Merkel explains how community centres by talented architects are transforming bad places into good ones and making good ones even better.

The failure of American public housing is so legendary that Charles Jencks used the 1972 demolition of slab blocks at Minoru Yamasaki's Pruitt-Igoe Housing in St Louis as a metaphor for what he called 'The Death of Modern Architecture' in the opening passages of *The Language of Post-Modern Architecture*.[1] He spoke too soon about the demise of the entire modern movement, but more than 25 years later publicly owned high-rise towers inspired by Le Corbusier's Voisin Plan are still coming down in Newark, Chicago and elsewhere, usually to be replaced by low-rise apartments and town houses like those built for the market in the suburbs – a model so land-intensive that only a fraction of the demolished units can be replaced.

In New York, public housing is an entirely different story. The only building that the New York City Housing Authority (NYCHA) has ever considered tearing down is a tower erected during the 1970s on poor landfill foundations at the Prospect Plaza Houses in Brooklyn, and all of its units are being replaced by the two- and three-family town houses being built around the edges of the block.

There has never been enough affordable housing in New York, so stable middle- and working-class families have sought apartments in complexes that only the poor would consider in other cities. And once they get one of these apartments, they stay – for an average of 17.3 years – several times longer than most Americans remain in their homes, especially rented ones. This stability became a boon to NYCHA projects when, in 1960, the US Congress established 'federal preferences' that decreed that all available apartments had to go, first, to participants in the Federal Witness Protection

programme; second, to victims of domestic violence; and, third, to people with only 30 per cent of the medium income – the poorest of the poor. These families, many of whom were troubled, quickly became the majority in the public housing in most American cities, and crime and vandalism rose dramatically. The desecration was so complete that, in the late 1990s, the ruling was reversed. Now 50 per cent of the apartments can be rented to people with up to 80 per cent of the medium income. In contrast, in New York, where the housing population is so stable, the very poor and dysfunctional always remained a manageable minority, and the ideal of mixed incomes that formed the foundation of the public housing programme in New York in 1934 prevailed.

Also, against all odds, the NYCHA's administrators and architects managed not only to maintain but to expand and improve its ageing stock of 181,486 apartments. Though it is probably about 600,000, no one knows exactly how many people live in the authority's 2,710 buildings because residents often take in relatives and do not report their presence, and so the unofficial population is always in flux. But the waiting list alone is larger than the population of most American cities (321,976 applicants as of 2000).

It can take as long as 12 years to secure a NYCHA home. One reason for this, of course, is that as moderately priced private housing becomes more scarce in New York City, the middle classes are more inclined than was previously the case to live in public housing in the NYCHA's 346 communities. Much of the credit for the attraction of this public housing goes to the director of design and capital improvement, David Burney, an architect who was born in Liverpool, studied architecture at the Edinburgh College of Art and then at the School of Architecture at Kingston. When he earned an MSc at the Bartlett, University of London, he studied space syntax with Bill Hillier. This theory, that space is based

on connectivity, draws on the findings of Claude
Lévi-Strauss and studies of spatial organisation
in primitive cultures. Burney also worked for
Shepard Epstein & Hunter in London for seven
or eight years, mostly on projects for universities,
and for Davis Brody in New York on the popular
Zeckendorf Towers on Union Square in
Manhattan. He once told an audience at the
Architectural League of New York: 'I used to have
to specify poor-quality materials because I was
doing luxury housing for developers, but now that
I'm in the public sector I can do it right because
we own it and know that we'll get our money
back in maintenance costs.'

Because of Burney's interest in research, the
NYCHA has undertaken comprehensive studies of
household composition and building security
with professors from local colleges. 'Dwelling
Design and Household Composition', by the
Pratt Institute for Community and Environmental
Development research team with Michael
Conard, was completed in 1997. The following
year it published 'Defensible Space Evaluated',
a study carried out with Columbia University
planning professor Richard Plunz, Michael
Sheridan and Michael Conard.

The latter study led to the replacement of hundreds
of building entrances. Now handsome stainless-steel
doorways and laminated-glass facades allow views in
and out. New reception desks, landscaping and other
features make the lobbies safer and more visually
pleasing at the same time. Burney's commitment to
design is also apparent in the new community centres
that the housing authority is building to fill up barren
plazas and keep young tenants productively busy,
and therefore out of trouble – an important goal when
42 per cent of the population is under 21.

Dazzling and Daring New Community Centres

Every year about $20 million of the NYCHA's $400
million construction budget goes into the building,
expansion or remodelling of community centres,
which are being designed by some of the city's most
respected architects and rising stars for communities
throughout its five boroughs. So far 15 centres have
been completed, another 25 are under construction
and 13 are in design, notes Eftihia (Effie) Tsitiridis,
deputy director of the NYCHA Architectural Division.

Although the programmes are similar, they vary
enormously in appearance. Agrest and Gandelsonas'
Melrose Houses Community Center in the Bronx,
near Yankee Stadium, is tucked into a silvery oval

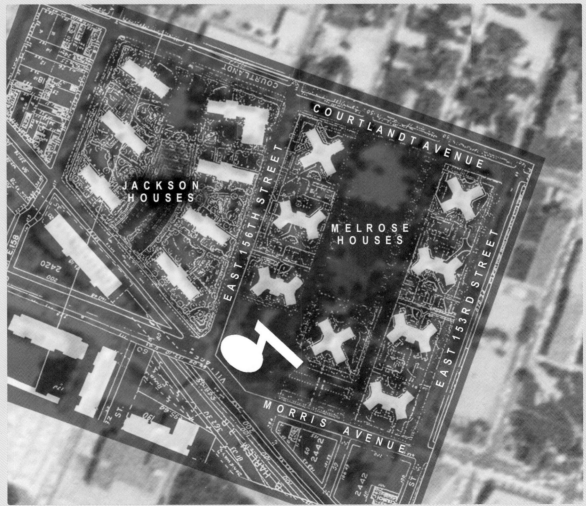

Opposite, above and right
Agrest and Gandelsonas, Melrose Houses Community Center, Bronx, New York, 2000
Designed with Wank Adams Slavin, this community centre has won half a dozen awards. Its gleaming-silver oval gymnasium is connected by a bridge to a long rectangular curtain-wall building for educational and artistic activities, including a recording studio, which was suggested by a 16-year-old girl from the neighbourhood who took part in the programming. The 20,000-square-foot complex is located on an open corner site that is visible from the train out of and into the city, and accessible to people from elsewhere in the neighbourhood who use it too.

JACKSON HOUSES

COURTLAND AVENUE

MELROSE HOUSES

EAST 156TH STREET

EAST 153RD STREET

MORRIS AVENUE

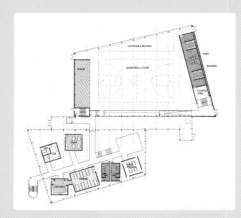

Above
Agrest and Gandelsonas and Hillier, Bruekelen Houses, Canarsie, New York (construction due to start in December 2003)

An atrium connects the two main activity areas at the community centre that the architects are currently designing for the Bruekelen Houses, while a bridge on the second level leads to each individual space. Aluminium-frame translucent glass curtain walls on the long north and south sides will be treated to provide for privacy and sun protection. Metal panel walls will sheath the shorter east and west ends. The outward-facing glass curtain wall, and an interior glass-wall facing the atrium, will be transparent. The centre is intended to tie tenement-type three- and seven-storey buildings to surrounding streets and provide a gathering place for the community's 4,000 residents.

made of standing-seam metal panels and a long rectangular 'bar building' with an insulated glass and anodised aluminium curtain wall. The oval gymnasium has a full-size basketball court, fitness centre and a stage for performances, connected by a bridge to a photo lab, arts and crafts rooms, recording studio and professional kitchen for meetings and a lunch programme in the 'bar building'.

Though the Willy Mays Community Center in northern Manhattan is the same size (20,000 square feet) and also tied to baseball history (it is located on the old Polo Grounds where the New York Giants used to play), it is composed of three colourful rectangles covered by a continuous standing-seam metal roof supported by long-span steel trusses. It was designed by Herbert Beckhard Frank Richlan & Associates, a successor firm of Marcel Breuer.

In Brooklyn, Oldhausen DuBois Architects built an unusually successful centre at the Van Dyke Houses with Weisz + Yoes Architects and landscape architect Ken Smith. 'It was the first to incorporate a design feature discovered in hospital research: people like to hang out in a large lobby,'

Burney said. In this centre a gently curved glass-walled public space serves as both a corridor and casual meeting place. An arc-shaped roof echoes the curve of the ceiling vault behind it and of the centre's plan.

Also in Brooklyn, Caples Jefferson Architects designed a centre at Marcus Garvey Village, a low-rise high-density community built with much fanfare in 1975 in a collaboration between Edward Logue's Urban Development Corporation and Peter Eisenman's Institute for Architecture and Urban Studies and exhibited at the Museum of Modern Art. Within a protected interior courtyard in the treacherous Brownsville area, two opaque, irregularly glazed masonry masses are linked by light, transparent, rectangular corridors, which together create another interior court.

At the nearby Saratoga Houses, City College dean George Ranalli used elongated bricks and elaborately detailed casting stone in a 3,500-square-foot community centre built into the base of a bland 16-storey tower. Mahogany window frames, folded plaster ceilings and clerestory windows give the new public spaces dignity and character.

Alexander Gorlin Architects took an opposite tack at the McKinley Houses in the Bronx. Here, a steel-and-glass addition visually lightens a massive six-building

Oldhausen DuBois, Weisz + Yoes and Ken Smith, Van Dyke Houses Community Center, Brownsville, Brooklyn, New York, 2001

Above and right
A series of gentle curves repeated in plan and elevation distinguishes the inviting, glass-walled design. An airy corridor that links the gym, study spaces and activity areas has become the place where people get together casually. And since kids going to the gym can see what's going on inside, some end up wandering into homework rooms or computer labs.

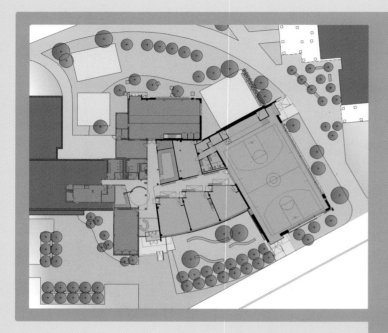

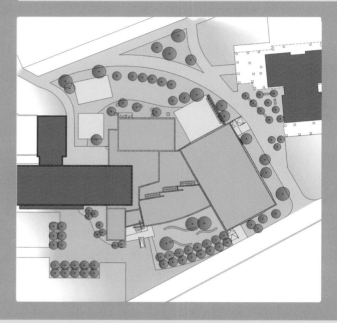

Thanhauser Esterson Kapell (TEK) Architects, Throgg's Neck Houses, Bronx, New York, due for completion in 2004

Above
While expanding an existing community centre built into the base of one of the 1969 Throgg's Neck Houses in the Bronx, the architects are tying the geometry of the complex back into the street system and away from the random geometry of the Ville Radieuse plan. The addition (consisting of a full-sized gymnasium, computer centre, classroom, weights room, ceramics studio and multipurpose rooms) fans out to accomplish the reorientation, while new landscaping and paving directs circulation around it and creates a new play area, senior seating areas and a basketball court. The small original gym is becoming an events room. To visually activate the box-like outer walls, the architects created overlapping layers of brick, glass-fibre-reinforced concrete, glass and perforated metal screens on steel armatures (which provide security at the windows). Interior walls are treated in the same manner with layers of finishes, applied screens and tectum panels.

complex. Its roof floats over the pavilion countering the weight of the surrounding brick towers. The 6,000-square-foot pavilion contains a multipurpose room that will be used as a theatre, auditorium, media space and games room. Also in the Bronx, NYCHA staff architects 'captured' breezeways and double-height spaces at Paul Rudolph's Davidson Houses in order to expand an existing community centre. Inside, they dropped 'clouds of light' from corridor ceilings that had been painted dark to camouflage exposed pipes.

Marpillero Pollak Architects is making the most of the 'park' around the towers at the Jacob Riis Houses where the architects are adding a multipurpose room to an existing underground community centre. Their trellis-like canopy cuts through the basement, opening it to light and integrating interior spaces with the mature landscaping outside. NYCHA in-house architects are also drawing on an existing Modernist landscape at the General Berry Houses on Staten Island where a new youth centre is designed as an extension of the landscape with a series of braced timber bents running through it, evoking an *allée* of trees.

An invited competition led to one of the most inspired new community centres at the housing authority's only International-style housing blocks. Designed by William Lescaze and other architects for the Public Works Administration in 1938, the long, low blocks of the Williamsburg Houses are arranged at a diagonal to the city grid. The winning design, by the late Wayne Berg of Pasanella + Klein Stolzman + Berg, was inspired not by the blocks themselves but by the visual transparency of chain-link fencing at the park next door. Like the park's ball courts, the Williamsburg Community Center is parallel to surrounding streets and has semitransparent walls and screens that offer views of what is going on inside.

Although the emphasis in most centres is on sports, many also have facilities for the arts and places where young people can get help with homework, prepare for high-school graduation equivalency exams and use computers. And one award-winning centre, Hanrahan + Meyers Architects' Red Hook Center for the Arts in Brooklyn (designed with Castro-Blanco Piscioneri) contains a public art gallery, performance space and art education centre in a building that is itself a work of art. The same architects are currently building an exquisite theatre at Latimer Gardens Community Center in Queens.

Pasanella + Klein Stolzman + Berg, Williamsburg Community Center, Brooklyn, New York, 2003

Above and right
Like the chain-link fencing in the park which surrounds it, the community centre provides views through its various activity areas. Only here, durable, inexpensive materials – glass curtain wall, glass block, Kalwall translucent panels, preformed metal panels, heavy gauge perforated screen, ground-face masonry units and exposed steel and concrete – are used elegantly. Their transparency not only makes the centre itself secure but turns it into a beacon at night, illuminating the park. A series of small pavilions, organised by function, extends from a central multipurpose space and spills out into the park, defining outdoor courtyards.

Top left and right
Intended to serve the 26 seven-storey buildings of the Bronxdale Houses and two other housing developments across Bruckner Expressway, the Bronxdale Community Center is located next to the expressway underpass. Designed by Sueyan Lee Kim of the NYCHA, it is a shell that splits open to form an open courtyard inside. An opaque field of zinc and ground face block shield the centre on the street side. The courtyard side is opened with glass. The shell dissolves at the corner into a glass box allowing visual and actual entry to the building and its courtyard. Using exterior materials inside further blurs the distinction between interior and exterior space.

Middle left and right
Because the eight six-storey General Berry Houses on Staten Island (construction due to start in September 2003) surround a large, oval, treed lawn, NYCHA architects David Resnick and Janice Camarillo designed the new youth centre as an extension of the landscape. The three-level concrete-and-masonry structure will emerge from the rock and trees at the base of Todt Hill between two residential buildings on axis with the oval. The new volume will have a wedge-like cleft through it, formed by braced timber bents that suggest an *allée*. The front wall will be fully glazed with doors that open on to the lower level of the plaza and overlook the central oval. A prominent stairway will lead to the main entry level with a lobby, director's office, large multipurpose room, kitchen and stage. On the upper level will be classrooms, an arts and crafts studio, library and computer room, dance studio and an informal gathering space.

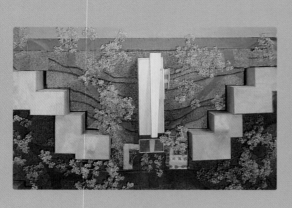

Bottom left and right
A canopy trellis runs through Marpillero Pollak Architects' Jacob Riis Houses Community Center, where a 4,500-square-foot multipurpose room is being added to the basement-level community centre, slicing through it and bringing in light, views and outdoor spaces. The connector is also a usable space, defined by the canopy trellis that has lighting of its own. The idea is to capitalise on the complex's open grassy areas with mature sycamore trees, planted in 1946 when the towers were built. Platforms and canopies integrate each indoor space with a corresponding exterior space, a strategy that not only makes the centre a nicer place to be but makes its activities visible to passers-by, attracting a new clientele.

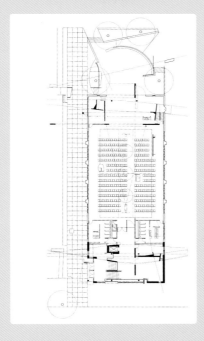

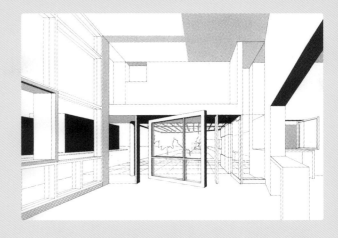

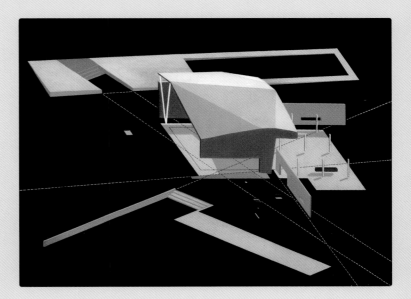

The idea of the community centre programme is not simply to improve the physical environments of the communities but to provide opportunities for their residents to develop talents and pursue interests they might never have known they had.

Renovating the Apartments

As a result of the NYCHA's 1997 household composition study, an ongoing programme of renovations is combining and reconfiguring apartments designed for single adults or two-parent families with children, but which now house single-parent families, extended families, residents with disabilities and people with other special needs. In 2002, 308 apartments in 27 different developments were adapted to accommodate people with disabilities in a $13.1 million effort that also included the installation of ramps and grab bars. While the emphasis in the community centre programme has been on youth, the next major undertaking will be geared to the elderly as many NYCHA projects have so many older people that they are 'naturally occurring

retirement communities'. The housing authority will not only have to make physical alterations but will also need to provide facilities for social services.

David Burney found that tenants were more willing to invite faculty members and students into their apartments than they were to talk openly with members of the housing authority staff who they feared had the power to evict them. And the Pratt team found that people simply have more stuff today than they did when the apartments were built, for example 54-inch TVs, bicycles, large music systems and many more clothes, so the NYCHA design department is trying to improve the closets and put in new sliding or swing doors instead of the old, easily breakable bi-fold doors. Tenants are also adapting their apartments to new conditions. 'The researchers found that a bedroom often doubles as an office or study room during the day and folds up into a bedroom at night,' Burney explained.

The biggest changes the NYCHA is making are at the Ingersoll and Whitman Houses near the Brooklyn Navy Yard, where the apartments are unusually small because they were designed for single workers during the Second World War. 'We are reconfiguring the apartments to make them larger,' Burney said. 'This results in the loss of one

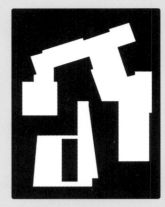

Caples Jefferson Architects, Marcus Garvey Houses, Brooklyn, New York, due for completion 2004

Even though the Marcus Garvey Houses in the Brownsville section of Brooklyn are a famous prime example of 'low-rise high-density' housing, crime in the neighbourhood made it necessary for the architects of the new community centre there to create a 'protected space' inside its courtyards where there was only 'a hard earth dog poop zone'. Caples Jefferson Architects developed a series of inner and outer courtyards with different characters and functions – a paved inner court and fountain, a grove of trees, a paved and shaded outer court, a playground and basketball court – together intended to activate surrounding exterior spaces. Two opaque irregular glazed-brick masses of heavy construction are linked with strict orthogonal corridors of light transparent construction. An east–west skylight interrupts the silhouette of the largest brick mass, making it the dominant light-gathering element in the meeting room. Within this precinct, an interior north–south courtyard creates a space for contemplation and gatherings for special events.

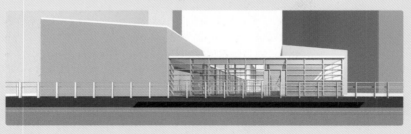

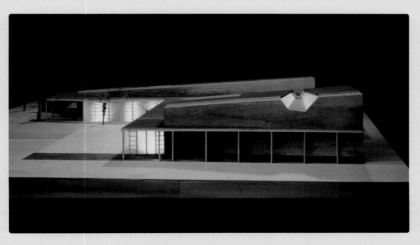

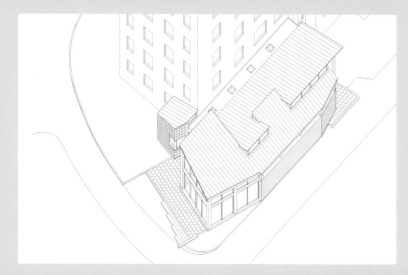

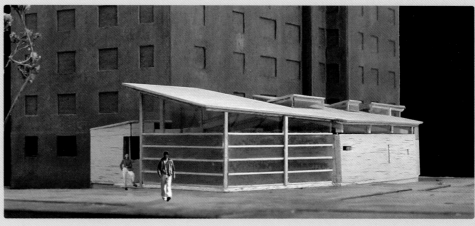

Alexander Gorlin Architects, McKinley Houses, Bronx, New York, due for completion 2004

At the McKinley Houses in the Bronx, Alexander Gorlin Architects treated the new community centre as a pavilion in a park. It has an interlocking roof system that reflects the idea of working together in a community and the contrast of materials between the heavy brick towers in the badly realised Corbusian 'Ville Radieuse' towers in the park, and the virtually freestanding pavilion of the multipurpose room of the centre. It is as visible and bright as possible so that the community is drawn to it. The light, transparent materials were selected to provide a contrast to the monotony of the surrounding brick apartment buildings, so that the activity rooms, theatre, athletic facilities and computer centre would look exciting and attractive.

apartment per floor so, in order to maintain the same number of units, we are adding two floors to each of the high-rise buildings and putting on pitched roofs. With land in such short supply I am trying to convince my superiors that we should go around adding more floors and putting pitched roofs on other buildings. Usually the structure can take the additional load and the pitched roofs are easier to maintain (and I think look better).'

Also at the Ingersoll and Whitman Houses, which are near Brooklyn's new commercial Metrotech Center, is a community centre that was built ad hoc over the years in a former retail space on Myrtle Avenue. In a renovation designed by David Resnick and Janice Camarillo of the NYCHA staff, the centre is being reglazed, expanded vertically (with a second storey) and horizontally (along the street) with a new two-storey gymnasium, while adjacent retail blocks are undergoing a $1.5 million remodelling for new shops and services that residents in the desolate towers-in-the-park communities desperately need.

The housing authority is also recovering street fronts wherever possible to tie the 'parks' where the towers are back into the street grid. At the Throgg's Neck Houses in the Bronx, Thanhauser Esterson Kapell (TEK) Architects is building an addition to an existing ground-level

centre that rotates the new spaces towards the street (and treats their facades as a tantalising collage). Sometimes the reorientation is accomplished by adding new housing, such as the 11-storey red-brick Sandra Thomas Apartments for senior citizens by James McCullar and Associates on West 91st Street, or with police service area buildings like the grey-striped one on Eighth Street and Avenue C on the Lower East Side of Manhattan by Boghan Pestka.

Past and present merge in Becker & Becker's new three-storey red-brick complex, called Lower East Side III, which looks for all the world like the authority's (and the nation's) First Houses on Third Street and Avenue A of 1934–5. 'What we've done in 65 years is come back to the beginning,' NYCHA spokesman Howard Marder observed. Both complexes open on to the street like old-fashioned row houses and tenement buildings did, with easy access to shopping, schools and transport, and yet they have secure green spaces in the rear for tenants to share – parks without the towers. But in the intervening years the New York City Housing Authority put into practice a whole series of experiments in housing design that turned out to be much more than tests of the latest theories. They've sheltered three generations of New Yorkers more humanely than has the public housing in any other American city, proving that contrary to evidence elsewhere, even now-discredited theories were not so wide of the mark. △

Architects as 'Housemakers' In Japan

Thomas Daniell gives the background to the 'housemaker' system in Japan, where modular homes are selected from catalogues produced by design-build companies. He explains how FOBA, the Kyoto-based architecture office of which he is a member, has developed an alternative model – branded for customer confidence as FOB Homes. Other architects, such as Mikan and C+A, are also diversifying the type, stretching its potential into do-it-yourself packages and spatial sampling.

Brand Recognition: Katsu Umebayashi's FOB Homes

A significant proportion of contemporary residential construction in Japan consists of generic mass-produced prefabricated houses. This is the world of the 'housemakers': huge marketing/design/construction companies such as Misawa Homes, Sekisui House or Panahome, themselves usually divisions of even larger corporations. Based on a set of modular plan typologies, every detail, fitting and finish is selected from enormous catalogues. Factory-fabricated components, including entire walls and entire bathrooms, are brought to site by truck and simply bolted together. Their marketing brochures invariably show Western-style houses isolated amongst lush gardens. In reality, they are likely to be ringed with narrow yards, windows facing directly into their neighbours' walls.

This is not 'social' housing; the target market is the affluent middle class, and these houses can cost more per square metre than an architect-designed home. Replacing Japan's traditional extended-family dwellings, they first appeared after the Second World War as the modern home for the salaryman + housewife nuclear family. They currently

every social class – was also essentially prefabricated, comprising dimensionally coordinated structural frames (timber post and beam) and modular infill elements (tatami mats, shoji screens, fusuma panels etc). Although related to the legal regulation of architectural aesthetics during much of the Edo period (circa 1600–1867), this standardisation was primarily an outcome of the insubstantiality of the basic building materials: wood, bamboo, clay and paper. Repairs had to be relatively fast and easy, whether the constant partial replacement due to weathering or the occasional total replacement after a fire or earthquake. The simplicity of construction also worked in reverse: traditional houses tended to be raised above the ground and without basements, and it was not uncommon for them to be taken apart and reassembled elsewhere.

While the ephemerality of the Japanese built environment is invariably explained as a Shinto-Buddhist acceptance of transience brutally enforced by regular natural disasters, after the Second World War it seems to have become a simple valorisation of newness (although not necessarily of novelty) for its own sake, symbolic of the nation's rapid

Despite the discomfort over these houses replacing traditional architecture and dominating new suburban development, there is a fundamental historical continuity involved.

account for 14 per cent of new residential construction, although the proportion has been steadily dropping over the last decade. More than 165,000 were produced last year (including prefab apartment buildings), each with an intended life span of three decades. This is house as consumer item: conventional, convenient and disposable.

Despite the discomfort over these houses replacing traditional architecture and dominating new suburban development, there is a fundamental historical continuity involved. Traditional residential construction in Japan – of

modernisation and increasing wealth. Traditional buildings may have required constant repairs, but contemporary ones are often replaced without good reason; land is worth less when there is a building on it than when it has been completely cleared.

Whatever the real reasons for this culture of constant replacement, it provided the conceptual basis for 'Metabolist' architecture, the Japanese contribution to the Megastructure themes that dominated architectural discourse during the late 1960s and early 1970s. The Metabolists' biological metaphors

---

Opposite
As seen in this example of a FOB Home Type A, the simple white volume is an attempt at a reserved neutrality rather than assertive Minimalism. Amidst the congestion of Japanese suburbia, this apparent insensitivity to context is in fact generosity: blank walls allow the neighbours to open their curtains.

Above left
Exterior spaces are contained within the main house volume, bringing in light and air while maintaining privacy. They are conceived as roofless rooms, continuous with the other spaces of the house.

Above right
The entire house is effectively a single, uninterrupted space. Air, light and sound are shared, with a corresponding loss of privacy. Every room seems to disappear around a corner, contributing to a feeling of spaciousness far greater than the actual floor area should allow.

may have been more a short-lived polemical statement than a plausible design strategy – the few built examples are scenographic rather than truly 'metabolic' – but they did provide an architectural language for some of the housemakers of the 1960s. Both Sekisui House and Misawa Home produced a number of pod- and capsule-based house prototypes, which market forces quickly transformed into simple boxes with pitched roofs. The Japanese public demanded a more recognisable image of 'home', and preferably one based on Western models.

Manifest in details such as the street-facing gable ends and side-hung windows, this Western influence extended to the internal planning: while prefabrication may be seen as consistent with tradition, the housemaker floor plans were unprecedented. The flexibly divided, multipurpose rooms of the traditional house have been replaced with solid walls and private rooms for each family member. Rather than, for example, a living area that is transformed into a communal sleeping area simply by the family rolling out their futons, housemaker plans are defined by n-LDK codes, where 'LDK' means living + dining + kitchen and 'n' is the number of

and the birth rate drops (symptomatic of a decline in the number of marriages), the perceived purpose of the house has shifted from a family shelter and symbol of social status to a comfortable retreat for indulging hobbies and entertaining friends. Land prices have dropped to two-thirds of what they were a decade ago, making homeownership available to a much wider range of people. The result is a potentially enormous client base dissatisfied with what the housemakers have to offer, yet wary of commissioning an architect – partly due to the profession's (often deserved) reputation for designing houses that are expensive, indulgent and dysfunctional.

At FOBA we had become acutely aware that building unique or experimental houses for wealthy or progressive clients is irrelevant to the general quality of housing in Japan. We had also learned that the decision to use a housemaker instead of an architect is not based so much on price or quality, but on the desire to fit in with the neighbourhood: for the average Japanese, employing an architect seems self-indulgent to the point of arrogance. While the housemaker houses are not seen as particularly high quality, their

bedrooms. This culturally alien emphasis on individuality has been identified by a number of Japanese architects and cultural critics as a contributing factor to contemporary juvenile delinquency and the phenomenon of *hikikomori* (people who stay confined to their rooms and avoid human contact).

Despite the housemakers' phenomenal success over the last few decades, they may prove too top heavy and inflexible to adjust to recent sociological and demographic shifts. As Japanese suburbia becomes saturated by these houses

advantage is the reassurance of ordinariness. They are like products from a convenience store: there are no surprises in content or price, and everyone else is buying the same thing. The gap between generic housmaker products and unique architect-designed houses seemed like a niche begging to be filled, as both business proposition and social vision. Beginning in 1999, we began to develop an alternative housing 'brand': FOB Homes.

The name has its origins in FOB Co-op, a Tokyo-based import company founded in 1981 by Japanese

Above left
In this example of a Type-B FOB Home, located outside Kyoto, notched windows oriented perpendicular to the facades allow light and air to enter without compromising privacy.

Middle left
Even in the contemporary Japanese house, shoes are always removed at the front door, and so FOB Homes have heating pipes cast into their polished concrete floors. The result is an impression of warmth even when the ambient air temperature is low, and a pleasant surface for children and pets to play on.

Middle right
The simplicity of the interior finishes is intended as a 'blank slate' awaiting personalisation by the inhabitants. The majority of belongings are kept in a large storeroom, and only the few items in constant use or display are in the main living areas.

Above right
In this smaller version of an FOB Homes Type A, located in Tokyo, a three-storey-high atrium brings light and air past a mid-level outdoor deck down to the lowest level of the house.

businesswoman Mitsue Masunaga. Established in order to bring European-made products to Japan, at that time dominated by American brands, FOB Co-op is now a nationwide chain of retail outlets selling household goods and fashion items.

In 1996, Katsu Umebayashi (Masunaga's nephew) founded FOBA, a Kyoto-based architectural practice. The shared name was originally due to no more than the family connection, but FOB Homes was initiated in 1999 as a joint venture: marketing to be done by FOB Co-op, design by FOBA. Based on Umebayashi's concepts, five prototype plans were developed, and a single house was built for a client in the suburbs of Osaka as a demonstration. Pamphlets and models have been placed in FOB Co-op stores, and prospective clients are referred to the FOBA office in Kyoto. While in reality they are dealing with a small architectural practice, there is the apparent reassurance of a 'nationally known brand'.

From the beginning, the emphasis was on marketing and logistics rather than new materials and construction techniques. We considered that inventing yet another prefabrication system would be an investment in methods that might become obsolete before any large-scale implementation was possible. The total flexibility of non-modular construction seemed far more promising. FOB Homes, therefore, can be made of anything, anyhow. It is only the spatial and aesthetic concepts that remain consistent. The preference is always for in-situ concrete, precisely because of its complete absence of any modular or dimensional restrictions, with steel or timber structures as low-budget alternatives. Although it is impossible to give accurate prices for the houses in advance (the design fee is fixed, but the construction costs are decided by tender), FOB Homes are generally about the same price per square metre as the average housemaker product. Cost efficiency is achieved by using the same few construction companies and consistent detailing.

Architecturally, the FOB Homes system is based on two principles: spatial continuity throughout the interior, and containment of external areas within the main volume. Interlocking L-shaped spaces (allowing every room to disappear around a corner) and courtyard gardens (conceived as roofless rooms) visible throughout the house result in a psychological, if not actual, spaciousness. The lack of clear room divisions and the resulting functional ambiguity is in many ways a shift back to a more traditional type of house. FOB Homes cannot be given n-LDK codes.

Visually, the FOB Home is a solid mass, a hermetic white volume filling its site. The apparent insensitivity to context is, in fact, a tremendous generosity. The blank external walls effectively 'donate' the surrounding yards to the neighbouring houses – if not as accessible space, at least as a huge increase in privacy (and therefore potential activity) inside and out. In at least one case, a neighbour regularly uses the adjacent white wall as a video projection screen for his own living room. While the stark facades might have been disturbing in an earlier era, within the visual chaos of contemporary urban Japan they are welcomed by the neighbours. There is even a historical precedent in the traditional *kura*, the white-plastered adobe storehouses that were fireproof annexes for wealthier houses.

The aesthetic was not conceived as a pristine Minimalism but simply an attempt to be as neutral as possible, with the almost inevitable result of a simple white box. This is intended only as a starting point, a basic frame to

accommodate the personality of the inhabitants; not coincidentally, two of the earliest FOB Homes clients were graphic designers, well aware they were being given a 'blank slate' rather than a finished composition. The typical FOB Home includes a large dedicated storeroom allowing the daily living areas to be kept empty of everything except the few items (books, CDs, furniture) in current use.

While the housemaker companies created an extensive network of factories, offices and showrooms before attempting to sell a single house, FOB Homes is expanding

Above left
Located near a busy multilane street in central Tokyo, there are no windows at all in the street facade of this tiny FOB Homes project.

Above right
Despite the lack of visible windows, the interior of the house is flooded with daylight. A strong relationship with the exterior is created while ensuring privacy and protection from noise pollution.

in a more fluid, tentative way; each successful project helps fund the next stage of development. Twelve houses and one apartment building have already been completed, another 25 are under way all across Japan, and we have had inquiries from potential clients as far afield as Zurich, Amsterdam, Las Vegas and Harare. Though FOB Homes was intended as a sideline to FOBA, it has begun to dominate the output of the office; it is possible that increasing demand will ultimately lead us to join forces with one of the housemakers.

The FOB Homes system is partly an attempt to reunite Modernist aesthetics (Minimalist white boxes) with Modernist ideology (democratic, affordable design). We here join a historical lineage comprised more of failure than success, whether due to co-option by a wealthy elite, as in the California Case Study Houses, or outright rejection by the intended inhabitants, as in Le Corbusier's Pessac housing estate. Perhaps only in Japan, where simplicity has always signified luxury, are such ambitions plausible.

Above
New Japanese suburbia is dominated by prefabricated housing based on Western models. Analogous to the imitation of Western clothing in Japan, there is always something not quite right; they are like inaccurate translations with surreal results.

Modular Coordination:
Kazuhiro Kojima's Space Blocks

The Kamishinjo Space Blocks project is located in central Osaka, an area of extremely high densities (although relatively low rise) with an equally intense mix of activities – bars, factories, warehouses, small shops and cheap apartments. The building comprises rental shops and apartments, filling every corner of its irregularly shaped site. It is contextual to the point of almost vanishing, comfortably integrated with its surroundings both programmatically and architecturally.

This is the first realised example of a design methodology that architect Kazuhiro Kojima (founder of Tokyo-based C+A) calls 'space blocks', a process of 'sampling' existing urban spaces, abstracting them into clusters of cubes (some exterior and some interior), which are then combined into new configurations. These various blocks interlock in a porous lattice somewhat like a three-dimensional version of the computer game Tetris.

The Kamashinjo project is based on a cubic module of 2.4 metres, resulting in relatively low and narrow spaces. The modules are linked in linear sequences, generally horizontally, sometimes vertically, and the integrity of the spatial system is preserved by using a structural system of load-bearing walls rather than columns and beams. Walls necessary for organisation but not structure have been made of concrete block, and so may be removed to allow for some spatial rearrangement in future.

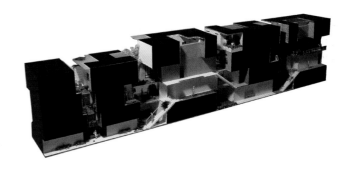

In 1999, Kojima and a group of his students began developing a 'space blocks' proposal for Hanoi, Vietnam. Initially intended for the '36 Streets' district of Hanoi's Old Town, the site was later shifted to the local Civil Engineering University campus. The starting point of the project is the traditional Vietnamese patio, here extended into a three-dimensional network of exterior spaces for the movement of light, air and people. With a 50:50 ratio of solid and void, the project manages to achieve density without congestion. Construction will be completed in mid-2003.

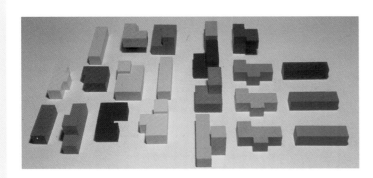

Top right (two images)
The Kamashinjo Space Blocks project is a mixture of apartments and shops that smoothly integrates with its context, both aesthetically and programmatically. The flexibility of the compositional system allows an opportunistic adaptation to any given site. The simplicity of the space blocks system results in a tremendous variety of internal spatial arrangements. Within the regular grid, every apartment may have a unique layout. A variety of family sizes is thereby accommodated.

Bottom left
The basic space blocks comprise between three and five connected cubes in a wide variety of spatial and functional arrangements. These are combined into larger compositions of porous volumes with a controlled balance of continuity and separation. The intention is to create an urban condition of density without congestion.

Middle and bottom right
The Hanoi Model project uses the space blocks system to extend the traditional Vietnamese patio into a three-dimensional network of exterior spaces for the movement of light, air and people. The research for this project was carried out by Kojima's students at Tokyo University, and received financial assistance from the Japanese Government. Construction began in 2002.

Do-It-Yourself: Mikan-Sei Homes

Mikan-Sei Homes is more of an organisational proposal than an architectural one. With almost complete freedom of scale, proportion and material, each project is adapted to the shape of its site (although the architects say that clients with irregularly shaped sites need not apply). The relationships between the house and the site – gardens, parking, windows – are decided in consultation with the clients.

The Mikan-Sei Home is divided into two volumes: the 'black box' (a cellular container of specific functions such as stairs, kitchens and bathrooms) and the 'white box' (a large, unpartitioned space). This latter component has a 2.5-metre ceiling height and no columns, with a structure of wood or steel depending on the overall width. Lights are hung from overhead beams and relocatable electric sockets set into a raised floor. The result is an open plan that permits ongoing modification.

The suggestion of the architects (Mikan, the Tokyo-based architectural practice founded by Kiwako Kamo, Masashi Sogabe, Masayoshi Takeuchi and Manuel Tardits in 1995) is to move into this open space unmodified, and live there for a while before making any decisions on partition and furniture layouts. They intend to act as consultants rather than designers, their guidance based on the clients' own desires. A range of examples of potential layouts is provided on their website. These include using ready-made furniture, Mikan-designed furniture, do-it-yourself interiors or employing a specific interior designer.

In Japanese, the project name contains a double-meaning: *mikansei* means 'made by Mikan', but could also be read as 'unfinished'.

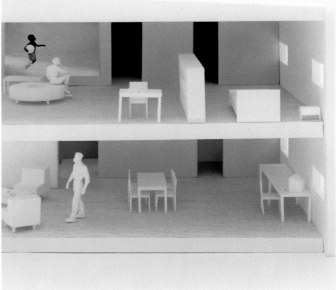

Bottom left and right
The Mikan-Sei Home is divided into two volumes: the 'black box' (a cellular container for specific functions) and the 'white box' (a large open space). This latter space is partitioned and furnished according to the client's preferences and in consultation with the architects. It is an open plan that permits ongoing modification.

Top right
The 'black box' and 'white box' are arranged in relationship to one another and to the site based on a variety of factors. These include overall proportions, sunlight orientation, privacy from neighbours and requirements for car parking or gardens.

Remake and Remix: Yasuyuki Okazaki's 9-Tsubo House

In 1952, in the context of a nation recovering from war devastation, architect Makoto Masuzawa (1925–90) designed and built his 'minimum house' – a timber-framed two-storey cube measuring 5.4 metres on each side. Masuzawa called it the '9-Tsubo House', *tsubo* being a traditional Japanese measure of area, equal to two tatami mats (approximately 3.3 square metres). The house footprint was 29.74 square metres (9 *tsubo*), and its total floor area 49.57 square metres.

Masuzawa defined four rules for the design of a 9-Tsubo House:
1. Square floor plan (5.4 x 5.4 m)   **2.** Ventilation area of three *tsubo* (3.6 x 2.7 m)
3. Cubic volume with gabled roof   **4.** Cylindrical columns.

Half a century later, in January 1999, the house was displayed as part of an exhibition at the Living Design Center in Tokyo. Shu Hagiwara, the organiser of the exhibition, was inspired to re-create the house for his own family of four. He bought land in Mitaka City (outside Tokyo), employed a builder, consulted Masuzawa's office (since the architect's death, his practice has continued under the same name), and had moved in to the new house by October 1999.

It was then discovered by Yasuyuki Okazaki, founder of Commdesign, a company selling designer products via the Internet, who decided the house was worthy of mass production as part of the Commdesign range. While refining the design in collaboration with interior architect Makoto Koizumi, he began developing a construction and marketing strategy.

Having turned the house into a polished 'remake', Okazaki then commissioned 'remixes' from eight contemporary architects using Masuzawa's original four rules. There was a major public presentation of the new designs at a symposium held in Tokyo's TN Probe gallery in October 2002. The remake and the remixes are all available on-line, as 'virtual' houses awaiting clients. Δ

Bottom left
The 'remixes' of the 9-Tsubo House. Based on the four rules established by Makoto Masuzawa, eight contemporary architects were invited to produce their own versions. These models were originally exhibited at TN Probe in Tokyo, and are now displayed on the Internet awaiting clients. Clockwise from top left: 'Tall' Remix by Hitoshi Abe; Remix by Takaharu and Yui Tezuka; 'Garage Life' Remix by Kentaro Yamamoto; 'Cellar House' Remix by Rikuo Nishimori.

Top right
Exterior view of the 'remake' of the 9-Tsubo House. The original was built in 1952 by architect Makoto Masuzawa, intended as a 'minimum dwelling'. It was shown as part of an exhibition at the Living Design Center in Tokyo in 1999, following which the curator built a replica for his own family.

Bottom right
Interior view of the 'remake' of the 9-Tsubo House.

ABBA Housing and Beyond:

The Future of Architect-Designed Residential Developments in Australia

At the top end of the market in Australia there has been a marked shift towards city living and higher-quality dwellings, which has only further emphasised the architectural desert of suburbia. Lindsay Johnston surveys the nadir that is moderate-income housing and illustrates some exceptions to the rule.

In Australia the myth of the people of the country is perpetuated by the cities that we have created. We live like farmers on our 150' X 50' blocks, kings (and queens) of our own domain. The car has allowed us to ignore the density necessary for a city to work logically
— Col Bandy[1]

The leading edge of architecture in Australia is the individual house – now widely recognisable on the world stage through the acclaim of Glenn Murcutt. Yet the sprawling suburbs of Australia remain largely untouched by an architect's hand, the worst Australian ugliness, as Robin Boyd wrote in 1968, 'Fediterranean' – nostalgic kitsch and 'ABBA – all bloody balustrades and arches', on houses now called 'McMansions'.[2] An encouraging trend is urban renewal with city apartment building at peak levels, some bringing contemporary and innovative designs that respond to place and climate. In the bush, generations of inappropriate aboriginal housing are being retrofitted in a socially responsive manner, and there are a few examples of creative new solutions. Alas in suburbia, good examples of low-density housing are almost nonexistent, while there are only a few isolated examples of ground-breaking medium-density low-rise integrated developments.

Australia now operates, like so many other nations in the world, under the glorious misconception that the 'market' will provide. A talk by the chair of the Australian Competition Commission a few years ago, to the National Council of the Royal Australian Institute of Architects (RAIA), foreshadowed the intention to deregulate the practice of architecture, allowing nonqualified plan drawers free access to the built environment and extolling the virtues of free competition on the basis that it was in the public interest. I asked, 'In the public interest – when? Now? In 10 years? In 50 years?.' There was no answer. 'Cheapest is best, today' seems to be the view – not the way to achieve buildings

of quality and wonderful cities of the future.

As little as 1.5 per cent of housing in Australia is funded by the public sector, leaving 'the market' to provide the other 98.5 per cent. Thus the great majority of housing is procured through commercial development, solely motivated by profit and with endemic conservatism. The result is that less than 10 per cent of dwellings in Australia – houses and apartments – are designed by architects. Those that are, with a few exceptions, get caught in the squeeze of a rushed, cheap design stage commissioned by commercial developers, often awarded on a fee bid or a free design knocked up by a few office juniors. There is little support for moderate and lower income groups and less privileged members of society.[3]

The international nostalgia of the 'the market' is pervasive, allowing consumers to enjoy car and product design of which Ferdinand Porsche would be proud, while demanding house styles with name tags such as 'The Buckingham' and 'The Sandringham' and architectural expressions to match; Eurocentric English village models with no shade, no ventilation, no eaves, dark roofs and the dreaded 'brick venereal' disease – totally unsuited to the climate and place.

The housing 'market' is a major engine of the Australian economy, driven by a population growth imperative fuelled by immigration. Ironically, one of the most visionary evaluations of the interface between urban growth and the natural environment has resulted from a Department of Immigration commissioned study from the CSIRO (Government Research Institute) entitled 'Future Dilemmas', which has evaluated population growth scenarios to 2050.[4] Currently, 79 per cent of Australians live in single detached dwellings, with 9 per cent in 'attached' houses and 12 per cent in apartments. There are 7 million dwellings in Australia today, and the

Opposite
Hully Liveris, 'Pintu Merah' – the Red Door, Darwin, Northern Territory, 2001. A private development of affordable apartments breaks away from the homogenised developer formula and responds to the hot and humid climate and architectural roots of this tropical frontier city with cross-ventilation and shaded balconies.

Right
Kerstin Thompson Architects, Napier Street Housing, Fitzroy, Melbourne, Victoria, 2002. In a more temperate climatic zone, this is an ingenuous inner-city dense urban block development of 11 interlocking three-storey houses incorporating integral garages, private ground-floor courtyards and roof terraces with 100 per cent site coverage.

study projects potential demand for between 2.5 and 4.5 million new single houses and 1.5 to 2.5 million new town houses and apartments in the next 50 years. Since 1940 the size of the average Australian metropolitan dwelling has grown from 100 to 150 square metres and this is predicted to grow further. The demand for land to satisfy these spectacular growth projections is alarming, potentially increasing the urban footprint from the present 10,000 square kilometres to between 12,000 and 15,000 square kilometres – land that really does not exist on the habitable coastal fringe of this vast but arid continent.

So, in Australia, there is an imminent crisis in housing that will force governments and housing bodies to look at ever more innovative design and procurement solutions, and new paradigms for urban living that move away from the 'big car, big block, big house', as described in a recent publication from the RAIA Urban Solutions, which concludes: 'Discernible conflicts are emerging between the need for change to meet these new needs, and the desire to preserve the familiar methods of urban development.'[5] Yet within the last five years there has been sparse publication of examples of group housing, other than top-of-the-market apartments, in leading journals *Architecture Australia* or *Architectural Review Australia*. Whereas in 1983 the RAIA could publish a book *Medium Density Housing in Australia*, with extensive examples by leading architects frequently procured by municipal or government

agencies, this sector appears to have stalled or been abandoned to the 'market' and nonarchitect designers.[6]

At the higher end of the market there has been a significant shift towards inner-city living, and state and local governments are developing new modes of partnering with private developers to achieve quality dwellings. There have been significant initiatives to elevate design standards through, for example, the contentious requirement in Sydney, introduced by the NSW state premier, that all apartment developments over three storeys must be designed by registered architects. Other initiatives include rigorous design review procedures, imposed by approval authorities, with expert panels that include highly regarded consultant architects. And several inner-city municipalities are now celebrating the emergence of new urban development paradigms using, in some cases, international architects partnering with quality Australian practices.[7]

In Sydney, urban renewal of old docklands produced such innovative apartments as Wilkinson Cadalepas's Pyrmont Point apartments (1996), and the 2000 Olympics created an opportunity for the development of the athletes' housing for later sale by leading developers Mirvac Lend Lease, as the Newington Apartments designed by HPA Architects with Bruce Eeles and Vote Associates. This opened up the Olympics venue as a new middle of the market residential area close to the urban hub and on a newly established transport infrastructure. Very much at the top of the market, leading architect Harry Seidler completed his spectacular inner-city tower Horizon Apartments (1998) and there is the residential component in Renzo Piano's signature Aurora Place (2000). In Melbourne, Nonda Katsalidis has set the pace with his early Melbourne Terrace (1994) and more recent developments such as the adaptive reuse Richmond Silos (1997) and Republic Apartments (1999).

Also in Melbourne, where the architecture has been notably more avant-garde than in Sydney, expansive residential developments are on the cards and spectacular projects include QVI Tower by John Wardle, QVII by McBride Charles Ryan, Eureka Tower by Fender Katsalidis and Victoria Square by Turner Associates with Europe-based Australian architect Peter Wilson of Bolles Wilson. In Brisbane, Europe-based Australian industrial designer Marc Newson is the signature on the proposed Llama apartment hotel. Sydney architects Engelen Moore have moved from being a small-projects practice to leading apartment designers and received a 2002 World Architecture Award for their Altair Apartments, which combine Minimalist 'new modern' aesthetics with carefully considered passive environmental strategies.

At a more affordable level, in Sydney, initiatives that have opened up development of inner-city urban land include the highly acclaimed apartment development at Moore Park Gardens, an old brewery site close to the Central Business District, by Allen Jack and Cottier (1997–2000). The expansive Green Square project just south of Sydney Central Station, driven by the establishment of the South Sydney Development Corporation, will be a huge residential community and early completions include the Nova Apartments by Turner Associates, now working on a later phase with Crone Nation and Bolles Wilson. Nearby, Stanisic Associates has a number of innovative slimline perimeter apartment buildings completed or in design, being undertaken by private developers but strongly mentored by the city council. Innovation in these apartment developments is driven by response to urban form combined with efforts to respond to climate with appropriate orientation, cross-ventilation, sun control and open-air living balconies. In the Northern Territory, Darwin architect Hully Liveris has produced an affordable studio apartment building that breaks away from the homogenised developer formula and responds to the climate and architectural roots of this tropical frontier city.[8]

Above
Lindsay and Kerry Clare, Cotton
Tree Housing, Maroochydore,
Sunshine Coast, Queensland,
1996. This seminal cluster
housing project, developed
collaboratively between
government and private
investors, explores
an architectural language
appropriate to climate and
place and achieves a fine
balance between shared
and private open spaces.

Opposite
Stanisic Associates and Turner
Associates, Atlas Apartments,
Alexandria, Sydney, New South
Wales, 2002. This ground-
breaking private development
of 112 inner-city apartments
brings a climatically responsive
'new modern' architecture
to an old industrial area with
single-loaded apartments
and double-level maisonettes
around a communal inner
courtyard.

Cotton Tree Housing, Maroochydore,
Queensland, completed 1996
Architects: Kerry and Lindsay Clare

Queensland's subtropical climate has given rise to a
distinctive architectural language that has an identifiable
Sunshine Coast 'school' fathered by Gabriel Poole who did
the early innovative group housing at The Hastings in
Noosa. Kerry and Lindsay Clare's Rainbow Shores
Housing (1991) demonstrated how a distinctively local and
climatically responsive architecture could be further
applied to group housing at 50 houses per hectare and
shared vehicle and pedestrian circulation.

The later Cotton Tree Housing has been informed by a
student project, and associated report 'Places of the
Coast',
in which Lindsay Clare participated. The project is located
on two parcels of adjoining land, one owned by the public
housing authority and the other privately owned. Clare
Design were engaged in parallel by both parties to design
an integrated development for both parcels, with some
public and some private houses that are unified in design,
materials and detail. Ownership boundaries were

realigned to facilitate retention of existing trees and
optimise the layout potential.

There are seven two-bedroom and one single-bedroom
dwelling in the private development, and two three-
bedroom, three two-bedroom and six single-bedroom
dwellings as public housing. The layout is orthogonal
and achieves a density of 65 houses per hectare using
the building elements to form vehicle/pedestrian courts,
courtyard gardens, private patios and decks with an
attractive overall village scale and character uncommon
in Australia. One-, two- and three-storey buildings rise
from north to south facilitating northern solar access.
The interiors draw from the many innovative private houses
designed by the Clares, and are spacious and usable given
the density of the site. The exquisite external building
details are strongly rooted in the seaside vernacular of
the region, providing layering, screening and shade that
moderate the intense climate while fostering ventilation
and blurring inside/outside boundaries.

Atlas Apartments, Power Avenue, Alexandria, Sydney,
New South Wales, completed 2002
Architects: Stanisic Associates and Turner Associates

Notes
1. Col Bandy, 'Postscript' in
Peter Freeman and Judy Vulker
(eds), *The Australian Dwelling*,
RAIA (Canberra), 1992, p 121.
2. Robin Boyd, *The Australian
Ugliness*, Penguin Books
(Ringwood, Victoria), 1968.
3. Angelo Candalepas, 'The
Collective Consciousness',
*Architectural Review Australia
– Residential 2000*, Niche
(Melbourne), 2000, pp 76–81.
4. Barney Foran and Franzi
Poldy, *Future Dilemmas:
Options to 2050 for Australia's
Population, Technology,*

A private 'for sale' development built on a former industrial site in an inner suburb of Sydney, 5 kilometres from the GPO building, this innovative apartment development was free of restrictive aesthetic conservation measures that often cripple new developments. The project consists of 112 apartments and maisonettes at four to six storeys over shops and cafés on a site area of 5,220 square metres at a plot ratio of 1.75:1. The architectural language is an interesting blend of 'new modern' and 'green', with strategic responses to orientation, private and public open space and availability of cross-ventilation driving the architectural diagram.

Occupying most of a rectangular urban block overlooking an attractive public park with mature trees, the 'thin' apartments are built in a street-based form close to the property boundaries on four sides, picking up the rhythm of nearby terraces, around a secure inner-courtyard precinct where solar access is maximised by varying block heights. A mix of apartments, lofts and maisonettes has generous external private balconies or terraces accessed by an inventive arrangement of communal and private stairs, enclosed glazed galleries and courtyard stairs. Only one building has a lift and open gallery access.

The buildings have a distinctive functional, robust appearance with strong grids, solid corner elements and interesting shaded double-height spaces. Apartment layouts have a strong environmental agenda utilising passive design to reduce energy consumption. Living areas and attached outdoor spaces are orientated to the north, east and west for solar access with dual aspects to facilitate cross-ventilation and access to natural light. Air conditioning and double-loaded corridors have been eliminated. Bathrooms are located on exterior walls to avoid mechanical ventilation. Shading overhangs, sun hoods, sliding operable aluminium shutters and internal blinds create a striking climatically responsive layering to the elevations.

Relatively low embodied energy construction of concrete slabs and concrete walls, poured in patent preformed panels, gives good thermal mass to moderate external temperature fluctuations. The central courtyard is designed as a bio-sink and utilises recycled roof water for irrigation, and parking is provided in a sub-basement car park.

95

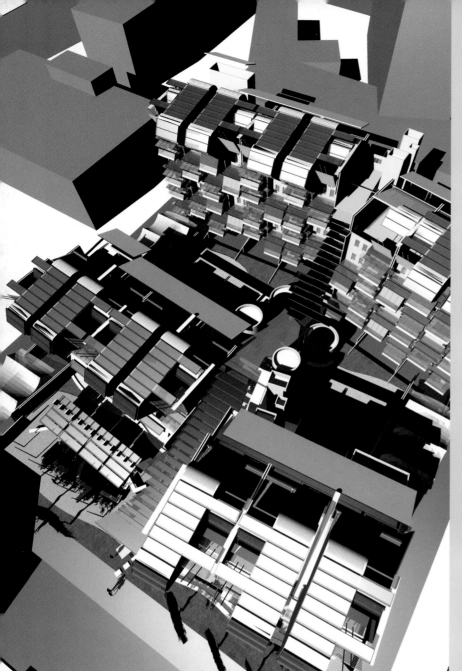

Raleigh Street Apartments
St Kilda, Melbourne, Victoria, designed 2001
Architects: Design Inc

The planned Raleigh Street Housing Development in St Kilda, Melbourne, is somewhat of a rarity as it is to be funded by the state government and was awarded following a properly constituted architectural competition in 2001. Authors of the brief for the competition included Robert Vale (of *Autonomous House* fame) who overlayed a rigorous environmental agenda that sought zero CO_2 emissions, reduction of water consumption to 50 per cent of current levels and a design life of 200 years. Over 40 architectural practices submitted proposals and the competition was won by the Melbourne office of architects Design Inc with spectacular proposals demonstrating a fresh and innovative architectural language.

The site area is 4,838 square metres and incorporates 60 one-bedroom units of 55 square metres and 40 two-bedroom units of 85 square metres. The development is separated into four buildings skewed to avoid direct overlooking and improve solar access. Each building is single loaded for cross-ventilation. The highest buildings are seven storeys plus two-storey roof-top pod maisonettes over a semibasement parking

area. Primary construction is of insulated tilt-up concrete sandwich panels and precast floors. Secondary construction elements are of lightweight renewable and recyclable materials.

All living rooms achieve optimal winter solar-gain and windows are shaded from summer sun. Many units have a novel solar balcony, which allows climate modification between internal and external conditions. The heavyweight construction is exposed internally to emit night-time warmth in winter and daytime cooling in summer. A service cavity in the party walls is used to ventilate internal bathrooms and eject heat from refrigerators.

A novel feature of the competition-winning project was the proposal to use a solar-powered on-site micro turbine generator to produce electricity and by-product hot water. Due to technical question marks, this has now been revised out in favour of solar photovoltaics and solar water heating. Passive solar design eliminates the need for winter heating or summer air conditioning. Low-energy equipment and lighting have been specified throughout. Energy demand for the apartments is calculated at under 5 kWh a day excluding water heating. On-site water harvesting, conservation and reuse is projected to reduce water importation to under 10 per cent of conventional levels.

Above and opposite
Design Inc, Raleigh Street Apartments, St Kilda, Melbourne, Victoria, 2001. Challenged by a rigorous brief that sought zero carbon emissions, reduction of water consumption by 50 per cent and a 200-year life, this public-housing project explores new architectural territory.

Resources and Environment, CSIRO (Canberra), 2002, pp 74–9.
5. Robert McGauran (ed), *Urban Solutions: Propositions for the Future Australian City*, RAIA (Canberra), 2002.
6. Bruce Judd and John Dean (eds), *Medium Density Housing in Australia*, RAIA (Canberra), 1983.
7. Chris Johnson and Margaret Petrykowski, 'Places for People', *RAIA NSW Architecture Bulletin*, RAIA (Sydney), Jan/Feb 2003, p 8.
8. Peter Fletcher, 'Pintu Merah, Darwin by Hully Liveris', *Architectural Review Australia - Residential 2002*, Niche (Melbourne), pp 82–7.
9. Lindsay Johnston, 'Victorian Sustainable Housing Competition', *Architectural Review Australia - Residential 2002*, Niche (Melbourne), pp 116–23.
10. David Brown, 'Moderate Income Housing: a Business Opportunity', *RAIA NSW Architecture Bulletin*, RAIA (Sydney), Jan/Feb 2003, pp 21–3.
11. Michael Keniger, 'Cotton Tree Housing, Maroochydore by Clare Design', *Architecture Australia*, Architecture Media (Melbourne), July/Aug 1996, pp 58–63.
12. Shane Murray, 'Napier Street Housing, Fitzroy, Melbourne by Kirsten Thompson', *Architecture Australia*, Architecture Media (Melbourne), March/April 2002, pp 50–5.
13. Paul Memmott and Catherine Chambers, 'Galiwin'ku Aboriginal Housing, Arnhem Land, Northern Territory by Troppo Architects', *Architectural Review Australia - Residential 2002*, Niche (Melbourne), pp 88–95.
14. Paul Memmott and Karl Eckermann, 'Jeannie Barney Court Housing, Hill End, Brisbane by Gall and Medek', *Architectural Review Australia*, Niche (Melbourne), No 75, Autumn 2001, pp 96–101.
15. Peter Hyatt, 'Capricorn 151 by Gabriel Poole', *Local Heroes - Architects of Australia's Sunshine Coast*, Craftsman House (Sydney), 2001, pp 106–9.
16. David Brown, op cit, pp 21–3.

There are a few examples of social apartment developments being wholly or partially funded by the public sector. In Victoria, the state government is progressing with plans to build an innovative 'environmentally sustainable' development of 100 apartments in the Melbourne suburb of St Kilda, the result of a design competition (the brief for which was written by Robert Vale of *Autonomous House* fame), won by architects Design Inc.[9] Also in St Kilda, Williams Boag has designed a development of 236 apartments, on a municipal council depot site, that endeavours to create attractive public and semiprivate spaces, and pays careful attention to passive environmental design, water management and reduction in greenhouse gas emissions.

Outside of the apartment sector, progress towards innovative solutions is slower. Former RAIA president David Brown has identified that demographics indicate a growing future segment of 'moderate'-income groups who will need to be housed, and that this may be a bigger slice of the pie than the saturated top of the market. Here lies the group-housing family market with increased densities and, potentially, lower sales tags. Design standards in this segment are, however, currently largely driven by customers' aspirations to have smaller versions of the 'McMansions'.[10]

Of the few innovative examples of group housing, stand-outs include the early work by Gabriel Poole at The Hastings in the seaside town of Noosa, Queensland, and the work of Kerry and Lindsay Clare at Rainbow Shores (1991) and Cotton Tree (1996),[11] both also in Queensland, and their recent group housing at Maroubra south of Sydney (2003). In Melbourne, Kerstin Thompson has produced a small, innovative, tight urban cluster development in inner-city Fitzroy[12] and, in Queensland, Troppo Architects and Bligh Voller Nield have produced a cluster development of 1,100 single-occupancy units for the army that explores a radically innovative architectural language.

The contentious issue of housing for the Aboriginal and Torres Strait islander communities has eventually received some attention by committed architects. Paul Pholeros and Healthhabitat, a group consisting of a thoracic physician, anthropologist and environmental health specialist, have implemented a huge programme of engagement over 17 years with Aboriginal communities, working hands-on with them to resolve thousands of fundamental sanitation, safety and health issues and to upgrade poorly designed and built public housing. Examples of new housing for Aboriginal communities include the prototype 'Knockabout Walkabout' portable outback house by Peter Myers, the competition designs for the Papunya Region Pilot Housing Project, housing by Troppo Architects at Galiwin'ku in remote far-north Arnhem Land,[13] and culturally and environmentally responsive inner-city group housing for older indigenous residents by Gall and Medek in the Hill End suburb of Brisbane.[14]

Of the 79 per cent of dwellings that are individual, usually suburban, detached houses, only a handful are architect designed, and of these some win prizes and are widely published as typical of Australian residential architecture. The remainder are an architectural holocaust, with air-conditioning contractors queuing up to make the uninhabitable habitable. Occasional attempts by worthy architects to produce elegant and appropriate kit or 'off the peg' project homes include Gabriel Poole's Capricorn 151 series[15] followed by his Small House series and, under development, his Takeaway series. Nevertheless, the now famous Pettit and Sevitt homes designed by Ancher Mortlock and Woolley in the 1960s and 1970s, of which approximately 3,500 were built, have few descendants in today's housing marketplace.

'Accessible, affordable housing is essential to our economy. But the supply of appropriate housing is not keeping up with the increasing number of moderate income households.'
— RAIA Past-president David Brown[16] ⌂

Lucy Bullivant is an architectural critic, author and exhibition and conference curator. She is the guest-editor of this issue of *Architectural Design*, and contributes to the *Financial Times*, *Tate* magazine, *Archis*, *Domus*, *Icon*, *Building Design*, *a-matter*, *Metropolis* and *Indesign*. Exhibitions curated include 'Space Invaders: emerging UK architecture' (British Council, 2001), 'The near and the far, fixed and in flux' (XIX Milan Triennale, 1996) and 'Kid size: the material world of childhood (Vitra Design Museum, 1997). Conferences include '4dspace: the Challenge of Interactive Architecture', ICA, London, 2003, and 'Smart practices in a complex world', ICA, 1997. She lectures internationally.

Helen Castle is Editor of *Architectural Design*. Since joining the editorial staff at Wiley-Academy in 1999, she has steered the publication in a new direction. She has collaborated with Christian Küsters of CHK Design and Mariangela Palazzi Williams, Senior Production Editor at Wiley-Academy, on reformatting and redesigning the publication. Helen has a BA in Art History and Architecture from the University of East Anglia and an MSc in the History of Modern Architecture and Theory from the Bartlett.

Thomas Daniell is a practising architect, and has been a member of the Japanese architecture office FOBA since 1996. He studied at the Victoria University School of Architecture and the Kyoto University Graduate School of Engineering, and currently teaches part-time at Kyoto University and Kyoto Seika University. He is on the editorial board of the *Architectural Institute of Japan Journal* (Tokyo), and an editorial consultant for *Archis* (Amsterdam).

Deborah Gans and **Matthew Jelacic** are professors in architecture at the Pratt Institute and partners in the office Gans & Jelacic, whose work to date includes furniture and graphic design for public schools and transitional housing for the homeless, as well as a range of private domestic and institutional projects. Their ongoing development of disaster relief housing began in 1999 as one of an international group of winning entries in a competition for war-torn Kosovo sponsored by Architecture for Humanity with USAID, UNHCR and War Child, and has continued under their own impetus with additional funding received from the Keep Walking Fund of Johnny Walker in 2001. They have recently returned from field visits in Bosnia and a research stay at the International Centre for Refugee Studies at Oxford University.

Lindsay Johnston is a practising architect, teacher and writer. He has designed apartment developments, group housing, housing systems and many individual houses in the UK, Ireland and Australia. His innovative environmentally responsive designs have been awarded and internationally published. He is former Dean of the Faculty of Architecture at Newcastle, Australia.

Jayne Merkel is a contributing editor to *Architectural Design*, and is based in New York. For many years she was the editor of *Oculus* (the AIA journal for the New York chapter) as well as having a career as a critic, writer and teacher, for which in 2003 she is being awarded the AIA Institute Honors for Collaborative Achievement. She is currently writing and researching a monograph for Phaidon on the work of Eero Saarinen.

Ola Nylander has a PhD in architecture and is an architect with SAR MSA. In 2002 Wiley Academy published his book *The Architectural Properties of the Home*, in which he presented an analysis of nonmeasurable architectonic attributes that are indispensable to the quality of the home and the residents' perception of their dwellings.

Mark Prizeman is a London-based architect and lecturer. His practice designs and fabricates structures, and he teaches at the Architectural Association and the Royal College of Art. He has recently revised and updated his father's book *The British House – the Outside View*. An article on tents made by his students appeared in a previous issue of *Architectural Design*.

Rob Wilson is a curator, writer and architect who since 1999 has been exhibitions curator at the RIBA Gallery in London. He recently curated a season of exhibitions about UK housing, including: 'Coming Homes: 3.8 Million Reasons to Think about Housing' and 'Model Housing: From Mobile Home to Country House'. He is currently working on an exhibition questioning what is meant by 'sustainable community' in the context of the vast new housing developments, such as Thames Gateway, that are planned.

Below left and bottom right
Berke has been called a Minimalist, and some of her furniture benefits from reductive thinking. Doors conceal interior drawers, simplifying the elevation of a wooden dresser. However, her plank shelves on a steel-strap armature defy the stereotype of sterile Minimalist rooms, where clutter persists only behind closed doors.

Below right
The functional, evocative Metal Angle Bed, from a furniture line developed by architect Deborah Berke, incorporates built-in storage below the mattress. Adjustable hanging shades descend like theatrical scrim, for privacy.

Furniture Fair

A growing number of American architects dream of capturing some small sliver of the massive US home furnishings market. To the casual observer it might seem reasonable that these architects, who design houses, should have worthwhile ideas about how to fill them. However, jumping into the business is not a simple proposition, as **Craig Kellogg** discovered during a visit to the fashionable New York firm of Deborah Berke and Partners, Architects.

'They were always pushing us,' remembers Deborah Berke, the glamorous Manhattan architect who became internationally famous a few years ago during the fad for extreme Minimalism in New York. In particular she remembers one demanding client at the height of the craze, an abstract artist whose paintings were mostly grey. The man first commissioned her to configure a new apartment, then to design the furniture as well once he had rejected everything available on the market at the time. 'You would think that a set of stainless legs with a glass or marble top would be good enough,' Berke says. But it wasn't, and the results of their collaboration spoke for themselves. The award-winning finished project ended up on the cover of the American magazine *Interior Design*.

Three years ago, Berke and her interiors team decided to develop furniture design as a side business. But how? Reluctant to surrender control of the process, they rejected working with a major manufacturer like Cappellini or Steelcase. 'It was probably the most naive decision we made,' Berke says, 'but also the most satisfying.' Over an intense nine-month period her team conceived an entire collection in-house. 'We tackled the design thinking like architects. The metal and wood mimic ideas in architecture,' she explains.

Like her buildings, the finished pieces would be disarmingly ordinary. 'We're not Philippe Starck,' Berke says. Hundreds of ideas were discussed, as the team planned wall-mounted book shelves, night stands – even a toilet-paper holder. Once sketches were finalised, craftspeople produced prototypes of them at full scale, with only occasionally disastrous results. 'When you do something that way, you own it,' Berke says. 'The basement of my house in East Hampton is full of prototypes.'

A giant party was planned in May 2002, to introduce the new line during the International Contemporary Furniture Fair (ICFF), held annually in Manhattan. For the evening, Berke's 19th Street loft offices were transformed into a spotlighted gallery. 'The party wasn't just about the furniture,' she says. 'It was about the mood.' Her guests were impressed. They said, 'Wow.' They said, 'This stuff is great.' But those same people also told the team: 'You guys are ... crazy ... naive ... innocents.'

Berke was lucky that the collection's armless tufted chair proved popular. The design was born partly out of functional considerations. 'Because of the tufting,' Berke explains, 'you feel the comfort of the padding with your butt.' But probably equally important was the way it looked. 'That's the Ooooo factor,' says Stephen Brockman, one of the architects in the office, who was especially involved in developing the upholstery. With plain, square wooden legs and proportions reminiscent of Mies's Barcelona Chair, this piece in particular proved to be a hook that pulled people into learning more about the line. 'We didn't think about the fact that we needed a hook,' Brockman says.

In fact, the architects had not spent much time considering their ultimate customer and his needs. Berke says too much knowledge might have crippled the creative process. But, having neglected to perform any market research, the team was on thin ice. Take the example of the Metal Angle Bed, a sleek canopy model fitted with adjustable privacy shades. 'Everyone loves it,' says Berke, but 'nobody's ever going to buy it.'

Below
At the Conde-Lledo Soho loft, in Manhattan, Berke's firm designed the Work Table desk, which is topped with an aluminium honeycomb panel. Here her metal display shelf has a clear finish.

Bottom right
In the Conde-Lledo Midtown apartment, designed by Berke's office, Bellini Cab armchairs encircle the custom bronze-tube dining table. A matching coffee table, beyond, is paired with a Kagan sofa.

Fortunately, it costs nothing for the bed to remain in the line since new stock is produced only after orders are received.

The furniture is sold through architects and designers. So once team members had produced and distributed a small printed catalogue for the collection they sat back and waited for the phone to ring. Almost instantly there was a problem. Who would field those calls? Berke? Back in unfamiliar territory, she hired a pleasant woman with a knack for sales to answer the phone and take orders.

Old architecture clients have since become some of her most enthusiastic furniture customers, though an entirely different sort of audience was discovered in Nevada last January. Twelve pieces from the line were shown to the public in the context of Unit B, a furnished town house in the 'luxury golf community of Lake Las Vegas Resort'. The development is located in the desert about 25 minutes from Caesar's Palace and light years away from Berke's architectural aesthetic. Referring to the pictures, Brockman says he was amazed at how successfully the line's tables and chairs melted into the eclectic rooms among antiques, art and rural knick-knacks arranged by the interior designer John Gilmer, a friend of the firm.

Now, more than a year after its debut, the line has finally come into its own. But furniture sales are not the only benefit of the project, according to Berke. 'What it's also done,' she says, 'is brought a whole different group of people to us for architecture who may not have known that we were capable of this kind of thinking.' ⌂

Below
View from across the river. The massing of the building responds
to the scale of the urban grid and historic core of the city.

Court of Appeals
in Valdivia

Jeremy Melvin describes how at Valdivia in Chile, Enrique Browne has seized
the opportunity to rethink the programme for a vessel of justice. Integrating legal
aims with a broader sensibility to location, climate and culture, Browne's recently
completed court effectively suggests how architecture might start 'to assume an
active role in the engagement between law and society'.

Below left
Long section. A long, grand staircase rises almost
the full height of the building, symbolically linking
the different spaces and activities.

Below right
Cross section. The composition responds to environmental conditions, with
the cooler, south-facing side housing working spaces and the main public
spaces looking to the sunny north side (this is the southern hemisphere),
suitably shaded by deep roof eaves and louvres.

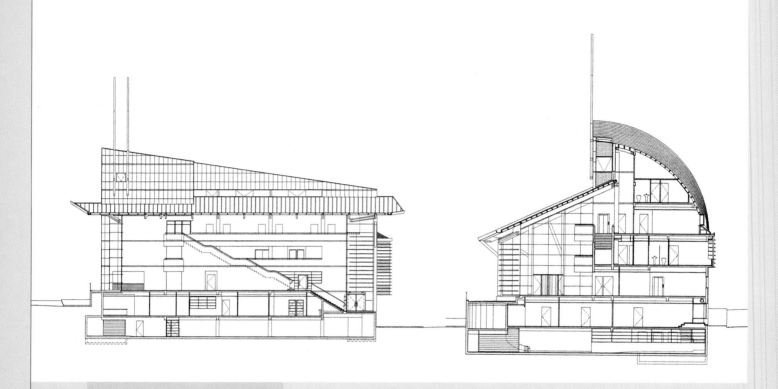

We may be grateful that justice is blind, but that is hardly an
excuse for architects to design law courts as if they were as
sightless as the goddess, leaving their designs to rely on the
clichés of convention to convey the majesty and dignity of the
law. But every so often an opportunity arises to rethink those
conventions and overhaul a legal system, and just occasionally
– Asplund's law courts extension in Gothenburg dating from
the early, heady days of Swedish social democracy come to
mind – an architect is on hand to give it visual expression.

Chilean architect Enrique Browne's Court of Appeals in
Valdivia, a city some 500 miles to the south of the country's
capital Santiago, is a more contemporary opportunity. Its
design addresses all the programmatic and civic functions
associated with a law court while striving for a visual idiom
that finds inspiration in the natural characteristics, traditions
and cultures of its location rather than extrapolating the
standard codes of law-court architecture. Here, for example,
the courtrooms themselves have magnificent views across the
river; litigants can have the support of family and friends as
well as their lawyers, and the overall form evokes the
familiarity of barn construction traditional to the area. Justice,
the thinking runs, is as much a part of everyday life as the
activities in any other public building.

Chile's return to democracy gave the country one of those
rare chances to remake its system of justice, not just to fulfil
the expectations of a liberal elite but to tackle some of the
country's fault lines which date back to the Spanish conquest
in the 16th century. The city of Valdivia itself was named
after the governor, Pedro de Valdivia, who died trying to
conquer the territory in 1553. He never reached the spot
where the city stands as the 'indigenous people were
too good at fighting,' says Browne, but the legacy of this
and subsequent incursions remains. The Valdivia legal
district covers a wide area and many of its inhabitants
come from indigenous communities whom the
traditional legal system put at a disadvantage even
without any discriminatory intent. 'It used to be all
written,' Browne explains, and 'a lot of the indigenous
people can't write.' On top of that, cases were 'very
slow, taking five, six or seven years', an imposition for
the litigants as well as many of the lawyers who come
from small towns across the district and had to find
somewhere to stay and work in the city. Today trials
should last only a matter of days.

These newly recognised programmatic requirements
set a pattern that Browne's design develops. He was
very keen to integrate the building with the city's public
spaces and institutions, and if the original proposal for
a plaza between the court and another public building
to the north was sacrificed for political reasons, the
composition still actively engages with the public. About
half its footprint is taken up with two triangular spaces,
one a small, outdoor, elevated plaza and the other an
internal three-storey hall. Its entrances from different

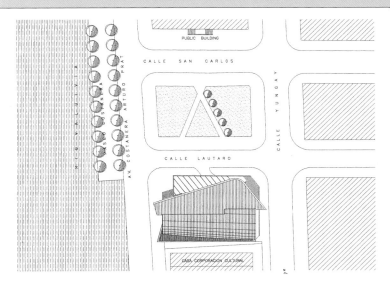

Original location plan. The Court of Appeals occupies a site defined by the city grid but also facing the River Valdivia. Early ideas for a plaza on the river between the court and another public building were abandoned.

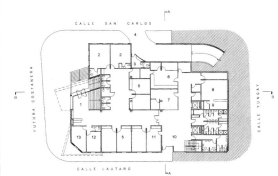

Basement: a change in level across the site gives the basement an entrance, leading to a grand stair up to the main ground level of the hall.

Key to plans

1   Public entrance and hall
2   Offices
3   Vehicular control
4   Vehicular access
5   Relator
6   Computers
7   Administrative offices
8   Cafeteria for staff
9   Kitchen
10 Judges' and employees' lobby
11 Special office
12 Offices
13 Lawyers
14 Outdoor plaza
15 Secretary
16 Principal courtroom
17 Meeting room
18 Senior judge's office
19 Chief of Personnel's office
20 Public information
21 Courtroom
22 Judge's offices
23 Library
24 Fax, copy machines, etc.
25 Machines

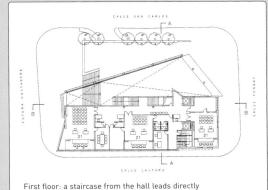

First floor: a staircase from the hall leads directly to the main court level, with three courtrooms.

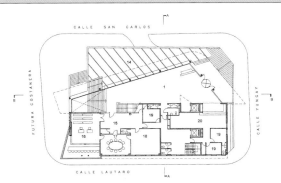

Ground floor: the entrance hall leads to the courtroom used by the president of the court, which enjoys views across the river. Only a glass wall divides the hall from a small raised plaza, symbolising the relationship between justice and the public for which the building strives.

Second floor: judges have one private level for their chambers, though its landing still overlooks the entrance hall.

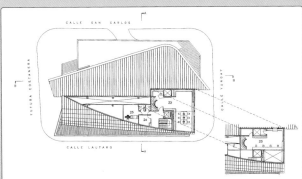

Third floor and mezzanine: within the flowing roof form is a small library, where lawyers and litigants can work if they have come from out of town.

Below
Using forms and patterns of movement, the design configures a new relationship between public space and the space of justice.

Bottom left
A traditional agricultural building, the roof form of which the court building 'remembers'.

Bottom right
The entrance hall combines drama with accessibility, suggesting the importance of law without being overtly intimidating.

Below
Interior of the principal courtroom. In keeping with the changes
intended to make legal proceedings less fearsome, the courtroom is
not a hermetically sealed container but offers views outside.

levels at either end invite penetration, while the glass wall to the plaza uses physical transparency to invoke the concept of transparent justice. Continuing the theme of using physical conditions to suggest conceptual ones, the president of the bench's courtroom is on this floor in a corner of the building looking towards the river; views across it make a backdrop to the judges for the lawyers, litigants and public. The message might be that justice may be blind, but it is accountable beyond the walls of the court.

One floor down, on the basement level, is the lower of the two public entrances with a flight of steps split either side of the glass wall, one part leading to the plaza and the other inside to the ground level.

On the floor above ground are three further courtrooms, one also with views across the river. On the second floor are 10 chambers for judges, and inhabiting the generous volume of the curving roof is a two-storey library. Here, lawyers from out of town can work during trials, an explicit symbol of engagement between legal processes, social need and a building form that, according to Browne, 'remembers' the local agricultural vernacular where large, curving roofs create big volumes.

Ideals like transparency and accessibility might even be expressed as abstractions on a par with the blindness of justice. They may help to set an agenda for architecture, but they do not define it, and that is probably about as far as the judges go; as Browne puts it, 'they were initially very conservative' and doubtful of some of his innovations. Yet after inauguration they became positive, showing how a specifically architectural sensibility might start to integrate legal aims with particular references to place, climate, culture and tradition; the design begins to weave an architectural 'metanarrative' that sets the context for the functional 'narrative' of legal practices. Architecture, in other words, starts to assume an active role in the engagement between law and society.

In Chile both nature and social realities are very visceral. With some of the world's highest mountains defining one side and the world's largest ocean the other, with its northern tip dissipating into tropical desert while 3,000 miles to the south its base disappears into the mists and winds of Cape Horn, it is a country defined within nature's extremes. Here, too, memories of dictatorship are still fresh, yet its history is not entirely negative.

Below
Finding the right massing for the building, to
respond to the site, climate and programme,
was explored through numerous study models.

Viewed in this light, Browne's design is a subtle synthesis of cultures, of nature and human artifice, of law and architecture. Manipulating a site that is recognisably one block of a gridded city within a European tradition, Browne also makes reference to the particularities of place, as the massing of the building responds to its historic neighbours. In using particular views the design responds to the uniqueness of nature in this place, rather than a concept of nature in abstract. And the roof form is not just a mnemonic of rural buildings and a practical way of dealing with the region's high winter rainfall but an integral part of the building's operation. Mixing the impressions of use with a strong visual repertoire, the design suggests that the new Chilean justice grows not just out of the soil of the country, but also from its recorded human history. To do this in a building that exudes optimism is quite an achievement. ∆

Duncan Lewis/ Scape Architecture

Known for their complex mosaic sampling of imagery, centred on the synthesis of landscape and architecture, Duncan Lewis's studio, Scape, based in Angers, France, is entering a new phase with the completion of its first major work. **Robin Wilson** explains how the high school at Fredrikstad, Norway, evolves Scape's vision for 'highly site-adjusted, often partially subterranean architectural bodies' through its sophisticated response to spatial and programmatic requirements.

High school at Fredrikstad, Norway
The Kvernhuset Ungdomsskole, the district high school of the south Norwegian town of Fredrikstad, was completed in the winter of 2003, with site work overseen by Pir-II Arkitektkontor from Trondheim. Much of it is seated within an excavated section of a granite protrusion. Its primary materials are the wood and rock displaced during the excavation – a reassembling of the existing matter of the site, bound with heavy-duty concrete. The glazed sections of the facades bear thermoplastic moulds by the artist Dominique Lamandé.

Previous page
Detail of a thermo-moulded plastic tree.

Below left
Classroom block facade detail.

The completion of a new high school (Kvernhuset Ungdomsskole) for the south Norwegian town of Fredrikstad in the winter of 2003 was the first full production of a building by Duncan Lewis since 1995, when he worked on the rapid assemblage of three low-budget rural gîtes at Jupilles in the Loire. But the work of his practice – currently operating under the name of Scape – had nevertheless been a frequent presence in the art and architectural press of mainland Europe in the intervening years. Indeed, project artwork has issued from his team's small office in Angers in such quantities that one would be forgiven for believing that Lewis's work had almost completely entered the realms of speculation and fantasy. As the new school testifies, however, nothing could be further from the truth. It is the work of a practice for which concrete material relations are paramount; a tenacious act of translation from the fluid game of cut and paste on the screen to the granitic geology of a Norwegian coastal town.

The glacial boulder-strewn and pine forest landscape of the edge of Fredrikstad was one of many diverse topographies to be fed into the distinctive image-making process of the Scape studio during the late 1990s. This quickly amounted to a transglobal series of propositions on the theme of landscape/architecture synthesis – the transformation of landscapes into host receptacles for highly site-adjusted, often partially subterranean architectural bodies. Projects have included exuberant visions for a marine park at Sochko, South

Korea, strategies for the preparation of the coastal plain of Qatar on the Persian Gulf for long-term development, and various cultural development schemes in their home regions of the Loire, such as a Parc du Végétal on the outskirts of Angers itself.

The imagery of the research and competition phases of Scape's projects is not simply produced in the cause of client relations; it is not a realist rhetoric. It is, rather, Lewis's means of commencing the aesthetic formulations that will ultimately be applied to the conditions and materials of the locale. Gathering photographic, mineral and vegetal evidence from a site fuels the production of imagery just as it will inform the production of the actual synthesised objects and terrains. The two are both products of a complex mosaic sampling, displacement and shift. Imagery of the envisioned project is not set up to be some mirror image to a final outcome. It is as much a simulation of the process of the future building as it is a simulation of its final appearance.

Lewis's reading of a site typically instigates oscillation and exchange between the totality and the fragment, often employing aerial views of landscapes to reveal the wider geographical dynamics that are obscure to the eye at ground level. The strategies employed have evolved from the need to shift rapidly

Below
Classroom block facade.

Below right
Detail of gabion block facade (arts and crafts).

between different scales of design task and diverse environmental contexts; to find an efficient means of extracting the material essence of place and converting it into the primary active components of design.

Two current projects – one in the process of being built, the other just emerging as phantasmic images from the screen – demonstrate well the degree of diversity. For a block of social housing at Mulhouse, northeast France, phagocytic cellular interpenetration was proposed as an analogy to the way in which Lewis's houses are to incorporate volumes of vegetation and integrate with the existing built environment (a 19th-century workers' town), learning from its vernacular oddities and gardening practices. Evolving the use of foliage envelopes used around the gîtes at Jupilles, vertical and horizontal mesh cages provide the supports for blocks of vegetation lying both within the interstices of the main volumes and demarcating functional spaces on and around the exterior of the buildings.

These analogous street-level equations shift up to regional scale for a project in Catalonia where Scape has been commissioned to produce visions and strategies for the transformation of entire river systems. The initial imagery (which will be displayed in an exhibition in Barcelona this summer) shows architectural and landscape systems that stage the high degree of material synthesis that has become central to Lewis's work but which are also to function as implants into the seasonal dynamics of the region. The master brief from the Catalonian government was to diversify and intensify land use, both in the higher reaches of the river canyons and on flood plains, tempering the annual extremes of flood and drought. Here Scape will be collaborating with XTH_Berlin, with which Lewis had previously worked during experimental workshops on industrial-scar landscapes in eastern Germany.

A further project, currently under construction and due for completion in 2004, takes as its material and topographical cue the vineyards of eastern France. In the centre of the town of Obernai, Scape is building a combined primary and nursery school complex and providing landscaping for a parking zone as part of the rehabilitation of degraded parkland. Work has begun with the shallow terracing of the site, which will then receive linear striations of integrated buildings and plantations. The aim is to import the geometry of agricultural landscapes at the edge of town into its centre. Three strips of classroom buildings, at varying levels of elevation from the ground, will be enveloped in foliage and linked by a central hall adapted from a standard pitched-roof greenhouse. Lewis's particular concern is to create a learning environment that has a high degree of porosity to climatic and seasonal change.

Below

Social housing, Mulhouse, northeast France

In the eastern French town of Mulhouse, Lewis, in collaboration with the Nantes-based design group Block, has been part of a coordinated effort with Jean Nouvel, Shigeru Ban, Lacaton and Vassal and Mathieu Poitevin to produce five separate strips of social housing, due for completion in summer 2003. The plot adjoins a 19th-century workers' town, which evolved from designs developed by the engineer Emile Muller in the 1850s. Budgets have been frugal and Lewis's design mixes a folding steel-tech structural system and high-grain Finnish ply cladding, with mesh-contained blocks of vertical and horizontal vegetation.

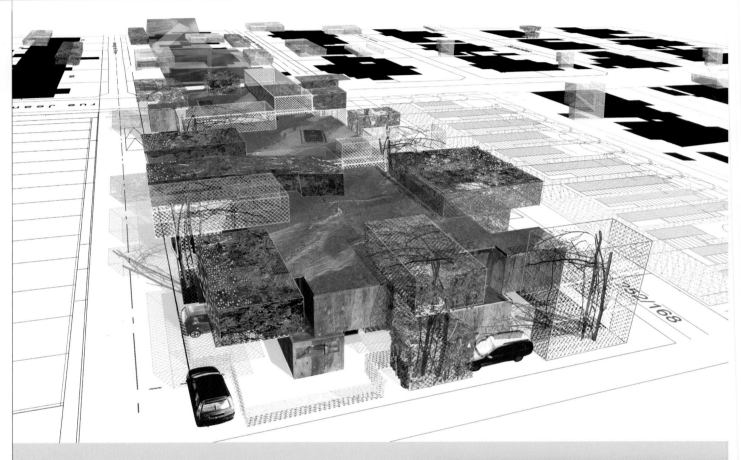

Granite Shuffle: Fredrikstad

In the transfunctional circulatory corridors of the Kvernhuset high school at Fredrikstad, it soon becomes clear that the forms and effects that dominated the imagery of the school as a proposition are merely the devices in an act of stage setting, of which the primary intentions were always spatial and programmatic. Perhaps the key achievement of the new school is, in fact, located in the fluidity of the mode of use and, indeed, of being it promotes. The school's physical intervention into the landscape is paralleled by an equivalent transformation of the psychological topography of the institution (the district high school).

Space for the ground floor of the school was excavated from a granite intrusion within the site. This also provided the material for the gabion blocks of the front elevation. Controlled, explosive cuts produced slabs and boulders that were then reassembled within the main ground-floor corridor, or 'canyon' as Lewis refers to it. Some have been worked to create occasional flat, utile surfaces, and concrete structural elements and staircases have also been strategically grafted on to the granite. The boulders pierce through the concrete and wood-wool ceiling, as do approximately 30 stripped pine trunks of the native woodlands, positioned intermittently along its entire length. Circular skylights occur randomly throughout

the ground floor, revealing the massive thickness of the structure – nearly a metre's worth of insulation, and a reinforced concrete that looks to be of military specification but is in fact a safeguard against heavy snow loads.

This 80-metre-long canyon/artery links a music room to the extreme east of the complex and arts and crafts workshops to the west. It flows through a restaurant space, the main foyer and reception, various shuttered concrete-seating niches and past the three stairwells to the upper level. It is a space, therefore, of constant interaction and movement, played out, playing through lightly processed versions of the mineral and vegetal elements of the landscape it has displaced.

Above the canyon is another east–west axis, with the library and computer rooms in its central sections. This in turn connects into the 'home bases'. These are the school's three classroom blocks, which run north to south, extending back into the edge of the woods, where meandering paths link through to wooden-clad suburban housing, the main catchment area for the school.

These strips of building interpenetrate with the woodlands. Two thin slices of forest have been left intact between them – boulder, lichen, root and pine

Below
Primary and nursery school complex at Obernai, eastern France
Due north of Mulhouse in Obernai, Scape is currently constructing a school complex with planted roofs and with facades of hydroponic panels, developed in collaboration with a local industrialist. In all, the panels will support 56 different species, with each of the three classroom blocks having different colour accents to their plantations. The intention is that

the project will establish a 'porosity' between the new buildings and the surrounding parkland, positioned in the centre of town, with the landscapes on the edge of town, from which Scape has appropriated the geometry of vine cultivation.

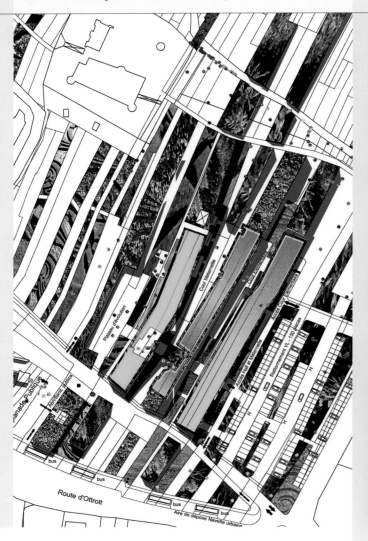

tree gardens simply created by the fact of their having been isolated and framed by the arrival of architecture. It is also at this intimate juncture of landscape and building that the associative play of the coloured facade elements is at its most active. Coloured glazing and thermo-moulded plastic trees cast from a pine trunk by the artist Dominique Lamandé will eventually appear on all elevations of the upper level. The trees effectively form two-way textured stained-glass columns, which from the home-base facades create colour signals that register deep into the woods and which play and layer across the views from within the classrooms.

Much of the complex work of assembling the school was overseen by the Norwegian group Pir-II Arkitektkontor from Trondheim. Site preparation involved the excavation of volumes for services from the granite core, and these now lie below and behind the ground-floor canyon. This included the drilling of 70-metre-deep boreholes. Intake ducts within the main front porch circulate air down into the boreholes where it takes on the constant temperature of the geological mass (approximately 15°C) before being circulated throughout the school to assist in the regulation of its ambient temperature.

The spring thaw will usher in a considerable transformation of the building and its relationship to landscape. It will to a much greater degree be visually reclaimed into the site by both the mineral (the re-emergence of surface rock formations from beneath the snow cover) and the vegetal – the first phase of foliage growth from plantation schemes that are intended to cover the roof of the ground floor and sections of the front elevation.

The imagery of Lewis's work is always of a state of architecture locked deep into context, bound into the tissue of the site. It represents some unspecified future moment of the building in its prime; some ideal phase of connectivity with the forces and matter of its environment. The work of the building of the school of Fredrikstad now continues through its relationship to time – seasonal, climatic and generational change. Erosion and mutation through time are anticipated in positive terms as the fulfilment of a designed quantity of fragility, anchored here against the exposed core and restructured mass of granite. ⚏

Studio Duncan Lewis/Scape Studio Duncan Lewis/Scape Studio Duncan Lewis/Scape Studio Duncan Lewis/Scape Studio Duncan Lewis/Scape Studio Duncan Lewis/Scape Studio Duncan Lewis/Scape Studio Duncan Lewis/Scape Studio Duncan Lewis/Scape Studio Duncan Lewis/Scape Studio Duncan Lewis/Scape Studio Duncan Lewis/Scape Studio Duncan Lewis/Scape Studio Duncan Lewis/Scape Studio Duncan Lewis/Scape Studio Duncan Lewis/Scape Studio Duncan Lewis/Scape Studio Duncan Lewis/Scape Studio Duncan Lewis/Scape Studio

Below
High school at Fredrikstad
Classroom block facade detail.

Résumé

Duncan Lewis/Scape Architecture

Mid-1990s	Collaborations with Jacques Hondelatte, Anne Lacaton and Jean Philippe Vassal, Edouard François and François Roche
1996	Establishment of studio in Angers, France
1997	Exhibited at 'Made in France', Centre Georges Pompidou, Paris Exhibited at 'Export', Institut Français d'Architecture (IFA), Paris Exhibited at 'Biennale Architecture', Sofia, Bulgaria
1998	Creation of Lewis/Potin Associates Exhibited at 'Premises', Guggenheim Museum Soho, New York Exhibited at Architectural Association, London
1999	Apartment block, Montpellier, France, in association Edouard François Exhibited at 2000 Biennale of Architecture, Venice
2000	Exhibited at IFA, Paris, Rushes 2
2001	High School, Fredrikstad, Norway, in association with PIR-II Tramway Station, Hérouville, France, in association with Tetrarc Water catchment station, Tours, France Study for a rural cultural centre, Louerre, France

Exhibited at 'Architecture and Geography', Institute of Contemporary Art and Architecture, Otras, Castello, Spain
Exhibited Social Housing project, Workers' City, Mulhouse, IFA, Paris
Exhibited at 'Archilab 2001', Orléans, France

2002	Creation of Scape Exhibited at 'Biennale of Architecture', Buenos Aires, Argentina
2003	Social Housing, Mulhouse, France, in association with Block Architects Nursery and primary school complex and parkland, Obernai, France School, Ornans, France Studies for social housing, Valencia, Spain, in collaboration with MVRDV, Actar Architectura, NL Architecture, Foa, Nomad, Frederico Soriano – Dolores Palacio Exhibited at 'Hiper Catalunya: Landscape and Urban Studies', in association with MVRDV, Actar Architectura, NL Architecture, Foa, Nomad, Frederico Soriano – Dolores Palacios

eifForm canopy, Amsterdam
The prototype canopy measured 12.85 x 23.3 metres, was 2.5 metres high at the south entrance, had a maximum height in the interior of 2.6 metres and reached ground level near the east wall and around the tree. The calculated design consisted of 132 unique structural members, 56 different joints and 74 unique panels. However, due to construction time limitations, the final built canopy dimensions measured 12.85 x 16.65 metres and consisted of 98 different length structural members, 40 unique joints and over 52 different panel sizes.

Generative Design

Blurring the Lines Between Architect, Engineer and Computer

Digital design tools can now be programmed in ways that enable them to generate various designs fitting within a given set of parameters, as described here by **Kristina Shea** in this fourth article of the 'Blurring the Lines' series. Far from automating and wresting control of the design process from architects and engineers, however, these types of tools engender an editorial role for them, at once freeing time for other tasks and also promoting a more thorough design study than would otherwise be achievable.

The Parametric Bridge
A post-design research exercise using computational optimisation
to automatically vary selected design variables within a parametric
model based on feedback from structural analysis while satisfying
parametric constraints related to fabrication methods.

Below
Deflection field for the optimally directed cable location
and bridge shape that minimises bridge deflection.
Bottom
Layered image illustrating variation in bridge shape and
cable location during the design optimisation process.

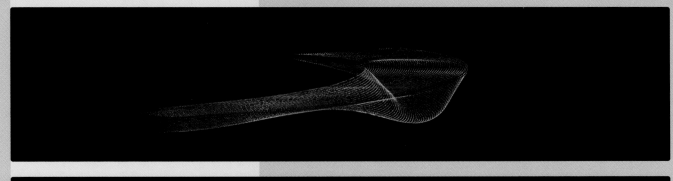

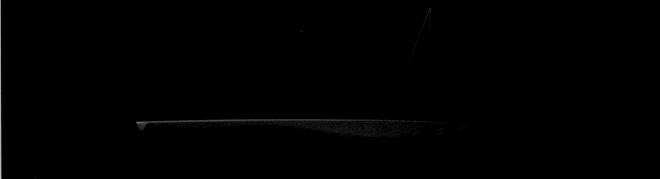

Imagine: as part of a project involving a cluster of buildings of complex geometry, several canopies need to be designed that connect different buildings to provide covered walkways and gathering points. Concept generation has begun and numerous schemes are proposed that vary where and how different buildings are to be connected. A CAD package with parametric capabilities is used to sketch outline shapes for the preferred schemes and develop parametric variants, which is easily carried out using the powers of associative geometry. The team then transfers these models to a generative design tool in order to rapidly explore alternative forms and structural breakdowns for the preferred canopy schemes. A generative model is created including design conditions such as material, usage, economy, construction and structural capacity considerations as well as selecting and creating design 'rules' that define a language of possible alternatives.

After experimenting with the generative model until most conditions are accounted for and the design rules appropriately reflect the style of variants the team wishes to achieve, a computational process is started to generate many equal-quality alternatives for each of the preferred schemes. The generative system quickly alters and evaluates thousands of design concepts, using the available distributed computing resources in the office when necessary. Finally, a few selected alternatives for each scheme are sent from the generative software directly to a 3-D printer for physical prototyping. At the design-team meeting the following day several alternative geometry and structural prototypes that meet the desired design conditions are ready for interpretation and further refinement. Fact or fiction? An emerging fact: generative design tools are targeted as the next phase in digital design.

CAD stands for computer aided, augmented and assisted design but not automated design! An integrated design process involving CAD, solid and parametric modelling, a range of analysis tools and rapid prototyping is maturing, and has been essential in the design of many unique projects. With the recent addition of parametric and associative geometry capabilities to CAD tools, they are now able to vary design concepts in step with designer intent, as discussed earlier in this series by Mark Burry (see *Architectural Design*, 'Surface Consciousness', Vol 73, No 2). Adding a computational optimiser to a parametric model shows great potential for rapid investigation of performance-driven design variants within the bounds of defined geometric constraint relations encoded in the parametric model. However, without designer intervention, which may entail starting the parametric model from scratch, the fundamental geometric constructs and their relations remain static.

Generative design is the next phase in digital design. Generative design tools are capable of generating concepts and stimulating solutions based on robust and rigorous models of design conditions, design languages and design performance. The computer now becomes a design generator in addition to its more conventional role as draughtsperson, visualiser, data checker and performance analyst. From a given starting point, generative methods introduce and erase geometry, components and features while maintaining parametric and topologic relations and constraints so that syntactically and semantically valid designs are produced. Incorporating performance models to guide the

Below left, top and bottom
The Genesis Generative Design System used here to generate Queen Anne houses and aircraft hydraulic systems.

Below right
Using shape-grammar interpreters for automotive styling. (Top) Generation of headlight designs from a field of emergent shapes. The shapes were generated from design rules based on brand image. A selected shape within the design field can be refined by the designer to produce a new headlight concept including turn signals and parking lights. (Bottom) Generation of current and designer-produced alternatives for a car front-end.

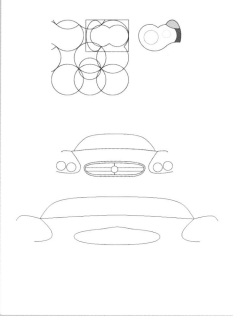

computational generation process will yield tools that help architects, designers and engineers think critically from different viewpoints, for example engineering performance, spatial performance, cost and fabrication, throughout design conception. This article gives an overview of the basis and future potential for generative design and issues surrounding integrating these new techniques within the design process. Using generative design tools, blurred lines and roles develop between designer and computer as well as architect and engineer.

Trends in CAD and analysis software show an increasing amount of automation mainly for routine tasks, for example code checking and the production of final drawings. Tool boxes can often resemble what are known as expert or knowledge-based systems, one of the first great success stories of artificial intelligence, that are aimed at performing routine design tasks, such as automatically configuring VAX computers, a now obsolete computing platform. However, knowledge changes fast. For example, the knowledge change-rate in the VAX example was about 40 per cent per year requiring a large, costly team of people to maintain the software. This does not seem a very viable option for a distributed industry like architecture, engineering and construction (AEC) outside of common tasks such as building code and consistency checking, and perhaps in cases where central control over knowledge is desired.

Moving beyond routine design tasks, can generative design methods impact creative design and further computer-aided creativity? It is commonly thought that the flow of CAD

technology stems from research and development in the aerospace and automotive industries and flows towards application in architecture, often as an aside. However, the contrary is true for generative design. Research in architecture has led to the first industrial applications of generative design systems in both aerospace and automotive design, not in architecture. Genesis, a generative design tool that allows interactive and automated generation of semantically correct complex 3-D designs, developed by Jeff Heisserman, was first created for the generation of Queen Anne houses and later found industrial application in the design of aircraft hydraulic systems.

Some commonalities between aircraft hydraulic systems and services engineering may exist. Genesis[1] is based on a grammatical design formalism. Shape grammars, a method for computational shape-generation, were developed as both an analytic and generative design formalism.[2] The rules in a shape grammar can be formulated to model a style of design, for example Queen Anne houses, so that only designs that are both syntactically correct and meaningful can be produced, called the design language. Building on shape grammars, development of a shape-grammar interpreter extends their usefulness in design as it enables a designer to draw the design 'rules' reflecting his or her personal style and design conditions that are

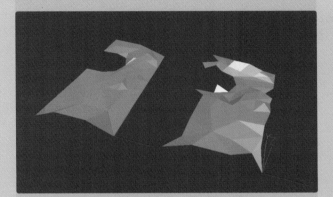

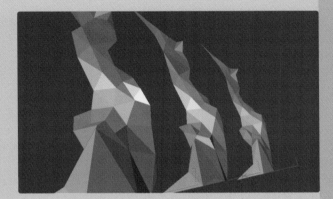

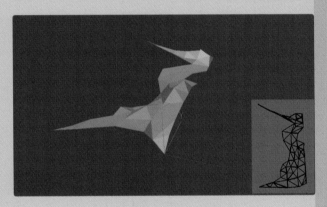

then interpreted by the software as the basis for shape
generation. This research is being applied in automotive design
for both inner hood panel and headlight design. In the latter
case generated designs are all within a shape language that
models the car-makers' brand image.[3]

To illustrate the potential for generative design tools,
perhaps even performance driven ones, in architectural design,
let us now explore the recent design of a courtyard installation
for an end-of-year party at the Academie van Bouwkunst in
Amsterdam.[4] The installation was a fused canopy and
landscape where the canopy became landscape by varying the
heights of the surfaces throughout the structure. This project
has elements in common with the initial scenario proposed in
this article. To add to the digital design experience, the canopy
was designed over the Internet by four people, myself (an
engineer and programmer) and three architects, in three
different locations, and then constructed in a week-long
workshop with architecture students from three countries.

The generative design system used to design the canopy is
called eifForm.[5] Given an initial seed design, eifForm develops
the overall spatial form of a lattice structure together with its
breakdown into discrete elements and joints (not necessarily
uniform), and finally sizes the individual members. To generate
both form and syntactically correct structure, a structural shape
grammar was developed based on traditional geodesic dome
patterns.[6] Structural shape rules are applied both backwards
and forwards adding and removing structural members in a

design while projecting the joints of the single-layer
structure on to a prescribed surface or to random
locations normal to a given ground plane to develop a
free-form faceted surface. In contrast to typical expert
systems, the power of a structural shape grammar is in
its topologic representation and parametric flexibility
that can be instantiated into exact geometry. Given the
desire to reproduce a Fuller dome we supply the precise
geometric parameters to a determined sequence of rules
while maintaining symmetry. However, when structural
rules are applied iteratively in random order and at
random locations in the design, the grammar defines
an infinite language of structural shapes including dome
designs conventional both in layout and geometry,
designs with standard layouts but new geometry and
new layouts that simply cover an arbitrary polygon.

Somewhere in this language, a set of designs exist
between exact Fuller replicas and completely random
triangulation. To direct the randomness of design
generation, we use a stochastic, that is,
nondeterministic, optimisation method called simulated
annealing that is based on an analogy to crystallisation
processes in the treatment of metals. The method is
capable of generating a set of equal-quality optimally
directed designs using rigorous performance models
that provide feedback related to the quality of designs
within the described language of alternatives. The

Below
eifForm skewed cantilever concept, London
Sparking research development by using prototype generative design tools in collaboration with practice. The lightweight complex geometry skewed cantilever shown serves to hold a nodus, located at its tip, approximately 4.6 metres from the building wall. The nodus casts a shadow on the etched building wall to provide a noon mark. The

design generation was driven by an extremely tight tip displacement requirement so as to accurately maintain the nodus position and thus the location of the noon mark. Equally visual lightness, which does not necessarily equate with structural lightness, was a driving design issue.

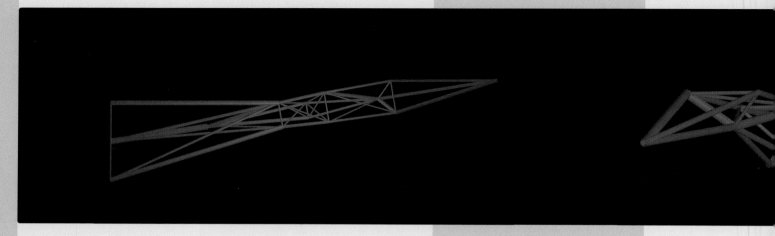

result is a generative process that produces nonorthogonal and nonplanar triangular-faceted structural forms that are purpose driven rather than just sculptural. Additionally, when compared to conventional structural topology optimisation methods, designer control over the style of design generated is now possible through the use of structural grammars.

The design conditions in the canopy project were developed iteratively through an ongoing collaborative team effort. The final parameters stemmed from usage, construction, economy and structural performance considerations. As construction time and budget were tight, construction conditions dominated the design and included limiting the number of structural members to 150, allowing only seven members to be attached at any joint, limiting the length of members to 2 to 3 metres, avoiding the tree area and using only two wood rectangular sections. Usage considerations constrained joint height to a maximum of 2.6 metres and kept the south and east edges of the canopy against the courtyard wall. Structural performance conditions included a material model of pine wood, an inexpensive and locally available material and a loading model that included self-weight of the pine members and covering material as well as live load.

The final free-form design consisted of 132 unique structural members, 56 different joints and 74 unique panels. It was a product of iterative refinement of the seed design, which was often a modified result from a prior generation process, and generative model throughout the design process. While the resulting design was not a dome structure, a relation between the structural patterns produced and geodesic patterns originally modelled is noticeable. The canopy design essentially does lie somewhere in between a Fuller replica and pure random triangulation. The randomness in the design is a product of the type of optimisation method used and the design team directing the series of generation processes adding, removing and modifying design conditions to use the generative process to sculpt the structural form. The series of generative models creates a form of documentation of evolving design intent throughout the project. While the generative design software was the core tool in the design process, it sat

alongside pencil and paper, CAD, cardboard models and the standard array of design gear.

Many issues arise when integrating generative design tools into the design process. In the canopy project described, the architects generally took a new role of interpreting forms, rather than creating and manipulating geometry explicitly. Generative design tools, especially those that include performance models, bring up new issues relating to authorship. Including both knowledge about desired style and of structural considerations, the computational generation process then becomes a negotiation between the two viewpoints. Blurred lines between the architect, conventional generator of form, structural engineer, conventional generator of structure, and computer are created.

Using the software in isolation, an architect may think that he or she can get rid of the structural engineer, since the generative tool becomes the 'expert' engineer and vice versa, but this interpretation is more akin to traditional expert systems and misses the main point. We aim to develop tools so that the architect will create forms that are more readily realised, for example structurally, and encoding rules of style and usage allows the structural designer to manipulate form within a common and formally defined language of design alternatives. Since the software itself contains only fundamental knowledge, for example how to put truss members together, both parties are needed to create effective generative models within which both the designers and computer then operate.

While an increasing number of engineers have a strong computing background, it is not likely that many designers, architects and engineers alike, will want to become skilled programmers. To get the most out of the potential of generative tools, architects, engineers and software developers will have to unite to create effective graphical interfaces so that design rules and conditions can be easily encoded and the generative methods themselves altered. However, consider that while it is not necessary to have been a stonemason to design with

stone, the experience gained when working directly with a material adds greatly to its effective and innovative use. This will be true, to some extent, when using generative- and optimising-design software. Black boxes will not do as design tools, and as such their effective use will be hindered. Computational design methods need to be as transparent and intuitive as possible. So, does this imply that computer expertise and even programming prowess will be included in the list of skills of the master builder in the 21st century? Perhaps just a hopeful thought from a software development perspective, but advances in scripting languages, graphical programming and design-grammar interpreters offer possibilities in the near future for designers to have a natural means to use generative systems.

Common to the creation of parametric models, encoding knowledge within a generative tool brings up questions not only of authorship but also of ownership. In the age of knowledge and intellectual property, who owns the encoded design knowledge within a generative system that is being shared in multidisciplinary and multi-office teams? Once it has been encoded, can it be used freely in the next project? Many issues surrounding the pedagogy and use of generative design tools remain to be resolved. Teaching of generative design has been under way at MIT for several years now by Terry Knight and others in the Design + Computation Group, Department of Architecture to understand these issues better.

The use of digital design tools will continue to increase, each having an impact on design trends and styles. Generative design tools are not intended to make every architect and engineer into Gehry or Eiffel reproductions but rather to allow them to formalise their own generative style, and operating within this design language rapidly generate and evaluate designs possibly with the additional aid of computational optimisation. As the development and use of generative design tools continues and is inspired by using the systems in their current research prototype states in both teaching and practice, we will continue to explore the issues brought forward. However, just to clarify, we will leave the possibility of computers designing and prototyping on their own accord for science-fiction books.

Architects and engineers will always be driving forces in the design process. It is just that as the use of digital design tools, particularly performance-based generative tools, becomes more and more essential, the traditional roles that have started to blur will continue to distort, offering great new design opportunities.

Notes
1. J Heisserman, 'Generative geometric design', *IEEE Computer Graphics and Applications*, 14 (2), 1994, pp 37–45. J Heisserman and R Mattikalli, 'Representing Relationships in Hierarchical Assemblies', Proceedings of DETC'98, ASME Design Engineering Technical Conferences, 13–16 September 1998, Atlanta, Georgia, US, DETC98/DFM-5749.
2. A critical discussion of generative design approaches, including shape grammars, can be found in T Knight and G Stiny, 'Classical and non-classical computation', *Architectural Research Quarterly*, 5 (4), 2001, pp 355–72. Further details on shape grammars are given in G Stiny and J Gips, 'The generative specification of painting and sculpture', in *Information Processing* 71, ed CV Frieman, North-Holland (Amsterdam), 1972.
3. J McCormack, J Cagan and C Vogel, 'Speaking the Buick language: capturing, understanding and exploring brand identity with shape grammars', *Design Studies*, in press.
4. For further description of the canopy design generation and construction, see K Shea, 'Digital canopy: high-end computation/low-tech construction', *Architectural Research Quarterly*, 6 (3), 2002, pp 230–45.
5. eifForm is research software currently under development by the author and her research team in the Engineering Design Centre at Cambridge. For further information about eifForm and using eifForm please contact the author.
6. K Shea and J Cagan, 'Innovative dome design: applying geodesic patterns with shape annealing', *Artificial Intelligence for Engineering Design, Analysis and Manufacturing*,11, 1997, pp 379–94.

Kristina Shea is a university lecturer in engineering design at Cambridge University and leads the Design Synthesis research group within the Engineering Design Centre (EDC). She is currently on a part-time Royal Academy of Engineering Industrial Secondment at Arup R+D, London. Her research and teaching in computational design focus on expanding the role of the computer in engineering and architectural design through the development of computational methods and innovative environments that support performance-based design generation and exploration.

The 'Blurring the Lines' series for 'Engineering Exegesis' is edited by André Chaszar, an engineer who combines independent practice in New York with research into cad-cam techniques.
   In the next article, André Chaszar will describe the potentials and problems arising with the development of integrated digital design tools, which are aimed at shortening the feedback loops involved in multidisciplinary projects and thus promoting collaborative design work.

Below
Josephine Baker from *Le Tumulte Noir* by Paul Colin (1892–1985).
Published by Éditions d'Art Succès Plate, early 20th century.

ART 1910–1939 DECO

John Outram, who designed the Pugin (1994) and Victorian Visions (2001) exhibitions for the V&A, gives the Art Deco exhibition a postmortem. Having not achieved the critical success of the Art Nouveau show, he wonders whether Art Deco's muddled curatorship and design is indicative of a broader malaise in the midst of an old friend.

The annual summer exhibition 'Art Deco 1910–1939', which opened at the Victoria & Albert Museum on 30 March 2003, is a critical shambles. Most journals review its contents as consumerist junk (*Sunday Times*). And none make much more sense than Tim Benton's conclusion, in his introductory essay to the exhibition's table-crusher catalogue, that Deco was 'all the greatest fun' (*Financial Times*). How has it been possible for the 'new' (cutting-edge black suit) regime of the V&A to reduce the first 40 years of the 20th century to an abject, intellectual, political and aesthetic shambles?

V&A museumology, even now, does not know the difference between curatorship and exhibitionship. Collections are for scholars and need no thematising. Exhibitions throw the net wider to attract people who have no intrinsic interest in the objects. Curators have to accept the unpalatable idea, at this point, that the public can be attracted in large numbers, and good broadsheet reviews obtained, only if the exhibition becomes possessed of a powerfully totalising narrative structure that the contents serve to 'enflesh' and make real.

Casson and Mann's exhibition design is the prime cause of the bad press reviews. Their layout of spaces is not designed to enflesh any coherent, totalising narrative through which the visitor can grasp the 'conceptual project' of the exhibition. Their 'spaces' are yet more of those tired 'open plan' gestures that were already indices of the 'decline of the West' when Mies made them at Barcelona.

Below
Foyer of the Strand Palace Hotel (1930s),
designed by Oliver P Bernard.

'The question of what distinguishes Art Deco from Modernism can be a tedious one, but maybe the assumption that Art Deco is always the intellectually poor relation needs to be challenged a bit more … let's hope that a new wave of original interpretative thinking is provoked by what is missing this time round.'
— Alan Powers, *Icon*, 2003[1]

How much longer do the 'space game' pages of this book of the death of architecture need to flop over to prove its shufflings are no more than a fan dance obscuring a view into nothing? The skin of this architectural vellum is that fashionable 'entropic sludge', a deep, dull, battleship grey, against which it is supposed 'objects sing' (although to God knows what melodic line).

The 'spaces' are denoted according to a set of the anodyne categories employed by curatorial taxonomies. We begin with 'sources'. These vary between the avant-garde, meso-America, Africa, Japan and diverse national traditions. Then the sludge-grey walls carelessly expose the Paris 1925 exhibition itself. At this point we have a whole room 'devoted' to the replication of the national pavilions that were, even then, replications of stereotypes of 'national character'. What is the point of a museum? What is the point of a major summer exhibition? Is it merely to be one more intellectually moribund replication of replications? When do we reach the point of an intelligent interpretation? A museum, especially in its major summer exhibitions, must progress beyond the level of junk shop. It must have attitude, point of view, a powerful political-historical-aesthetical narrative to narrate!

In the exhibition catalogue, Tim and Charlotte Benton introduce Art Deco architecture by questioning whether it is architecture at all and not merely 'decorated building'. What is the point of giving Art Deco to two critics who have that built-in Modernist-PC attitude that there is no architecture except the rejectionist anti-architecture of the Corbusier that they pretend, but fail, to understand? Do they know that the iconography of Art Deco extends that of *L'Age d'Or,* which underpinned the whole of the political project of the Western ideal state? Do they know that Corbusier himself, in *The Home of Man*, explicitly invoked this myth to his project? They surely know that Corb laboured for many years to become a decorative artist, failed to make the grade (like Loos he was incapable of designing ornament), travelled in the East and came back to propose the Pavillon d'Esprit Nouveau. At this point a trendy French politician, charmed by Corb's sloganising rhetoric, wanted to give him a prize. This was refused by the grand old man of French Modernism, Auguste Perret, who condemned Corb's pavilion by stating (very exactly) 'that there was no Architecture in it'.

The Bentons, like any English critics of Modernism, cannot be expected to understand, it seems, that the huge effort invested by the French state in creating a new 20th-century style was powered by the general project to create a rational state, with all of its aspects, from warfare, trade, philosophy, town planning and all of the trades and crafts that circulate money and bring revenue to the state. This 'ideal state' may have been reinvented (after a putatively Hellenic model), by the small despotisms of the Mediterranean Renaissance, but it found its first and brilliant exemplar, astonishing the European empires, under the English Tudors. The brilliance of a rationally governed state continued to power Britain forward until the French Revolution, and then Napoleon, caused Britain, under the influence of Metternich and Romanticism, to impose the neo-feudal fog that I, in my design for 'Victorian Visions 1838–1901' (V&A, summer 2001), explored with a sharply critical eye. The so-called 'Art Deco' period – 1910–39 – followed directly on from the period of my own exhibition design.

The 20th-century Modernism of first France and then the US, conceived before the First World War but flowering between those two 20th-century catastrophes, was a wonderfully complex phenomenon, genuinely global in scope, at home as much in Japan and India as in Australia and Argentina. This ravishing dawn of modernity was entirely rejected by the British Establishment who, even after 1918, basked in the sunset of empire. The British, secure on their sheep farms, and still possessed of most of the world's capital, preferred to relax in the thatched half-timbered bungalow palaces of Lutyens while going on parade behind his stylish imperial-baroque colonnades. The

Moderne was the style the British Establishment never had.

As France sank into yet another morass of continental politics, the torch of Modernity passed to the US – with such brilliant designers as Ely Jacques Kahn. (Here illustrated with a lousy 'box brownie' snap by Tim Benton.) American critics are correct in not using the term 'Deco'. It is a pejorative, first coined by Corbusier in 1925, but only established in 1968 by the entertaining dilettante Bevis Hillier to describe a new class of 'collectibles'. The term 'Deco' should be rejected by anyone with any pretensions to seriousness about 20th-century culture. American critics distinguish between pre- and post-1939–45 war styles by using 'Moderne' for the earlier and 'Modern' for the later.

The Moderne ought to be studied for its exposure of how necessary it proved to be able to fully decipher the Western artistic canon in order to renew it, as attempted by the pre-1939 war 'Moderne' rather than merely accept its total loss –

> 'With about 300 objects on display here, the difficulty of finding an umbrella definition for Art Deco is immediately apparent … London seems an unlikely place to hold this show. Art Deco was born in Paris and was most exuberant in the United States. But is was in the United States that Art Deco really took off.'
>
> — Alan Riding, *International Herald Tribune*, 2003[2]

as did the post-1939 war 'Modern'. At his 1912 Rome Conference, Aby Warburg proposed that art should no longer be understood via 19th-century formalisms and genres but through 20th-century iconographies and narratologies. This appeal failed in architecture and the fine arts. These became, over the 20 century, more formalised and even more iconically anti-literate.

The decorative arts, film and advertising fulfilled Warburg's project – albeit mainly in a relentlessly *jejeune* manner. But that is irrelevant. Nearly all artefacts lack style and quality. The role of museumology and criticism is not to evaluate 'taste' – that is for shopkeepers – but to create interpretations and understandings. The Moderne assimilated and extended all of the iconographies and narratologies of Western design.

Moreover, it reinvented them with a novelty drawn from a global diversity of formalities. The 19th-century failure of Western art was, above all else, the collapse of its perspectivised 'natural' space. The Moderne essayed, for the first time ever, to mediate the West's native iconic structures via the 'flat space' that one finds employed by all other artistic traditions. The Moderne tried to rectify a fundamental weakness in Western design – its inability to 'write coherently' on the surfaces of solid materials. How, for example, was it possible for Tim Benton to ignore Frank Lloyd Wright's Imperial Hotel in Japan, the most extended and brilliant essay in the Moderne of the whole period? Clearly he excludes Wright so that he can downgrade the whole movement and avoid exposing his native theoretical inadequacy when faced by a surface-scripted design medium.

The fact that this period failed to rectify this indigenous inadequacy of Western design was not a failure of *Homo faber*, the makers of the moderne, but a failure of *Homo sapiens*, the writers and theorists of Modernity, who failed to fabricate the theory and metaphysic required to renew the conceptual support that art and design always needs. Clement Greenberg's 1940s Minimalism is here not the prophylactic to the Western disease of iconic incapacity, but its symptom.

Conscious of their failure, it was the writers and theorists who went on to destroy the Moderne and replace it with the Modern. Hitchcock, Barr and Johnson, in 1932, showed the White Existenzminimum, International-style architecture at the Museum of Modern Art (MoMA). They drew forth a public street procession that wound through New York, capital of the Moderne. In it walked all the glorious craftspeople who had created their fabulous city. They were protesting against the iconic illiteracy of the failed metaphysicians who sought to inflate their own inadequacy into a dominant ethic.

The critical failure of the V&A's 'Art Deco 1910–1939' is just one more chapter in the fundamental weakness of the Modern – its continuing lack of an operationally effective theoretical purchase upon the actual phenomena of art and design. In the case of the V&A, the root cause of this inadequacy is obvious – the revolution in thinking required to build Alan Borg's 'spiral turd' extension. Until that project is abandoned, the V&A is doomed to its futile cult of 'good design' and the rejection of hard, truthful, historical thinking – especially in relation to totally alien projects like the Franco-American Moderne. Δ◻

Notes
1. Alan Powers, 'A Slice of Art History', *Icon*, May 2003.
2. Alan Riding, 'Escapism in Flashy Design', *International Herald Tribune*, 15 April 2003 (reprint from the *New York Times*).

Magnet

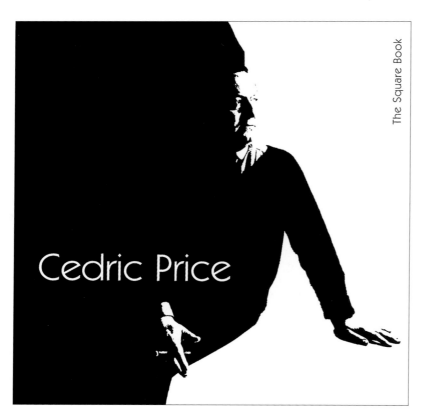

The Square Book

Cedric Price

In 2002 Cedric Price was awarded the Frederick Kiesler Prize. **Samantha Hardingham**, the editor of one of two books on Price published by Wiley-Academy, briefly summarises his contribution in a year that Archigram won the RIBA Gold Medal. She describes Magnet, Price's ongoing visionary project for Greater London.

It is appropriate and important that Cedric Price (1934) has been awarded the Frederick Kiesler Prize in 2002 for three good reasons. Firstly, it draws our attention to not one but two visionary architects from successive generations. Frederick Kiesler (1890–1965) and Price share 'a world infinitely remade and reconstructed, a world that is capable of infinite transmutation'.[1] Both talk of continuity, but not of sameness. Secondly, the prize has been awarded in the same year that Archigram has been awarded the RIBA Gold Medal. Although not a member of this group (and quite deliberately so), Price's writings and contributions to editions of *Archigram*, the magazine, were a key influence on the group's work in the 1960s. Warren Chalk of Archigram wrote:

> Of all my friends there have been three imaginers of note, of originality and wit, with something profound to say. Cedric Price is one. Ideas are precious and their source should be recognised, acknowledged and appreciated in the context of time.[2]

And thirdly, because it is not before time that the unique and heroic status that Price holds internationally within and without the architectural profession is being publicly acknowledged and congratulated.

Time, the fourth dimension in design, is Price's most treasured design tool. His is an architecture of 'beneficial change', an 'anticipatory architecture' that argues that

Below
Preliminary sketches for the Price's ten Magnets;
black ink and red pencil on A4 tissue paper.

Right
Cover, *Cedric Price Opera* (2003)

OPERA

EDITED BY SAMANTHA HARDINGHAM

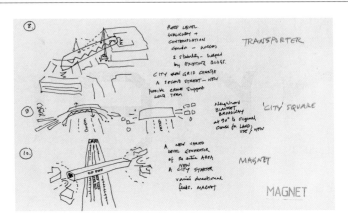

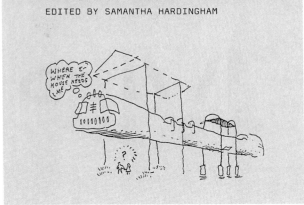

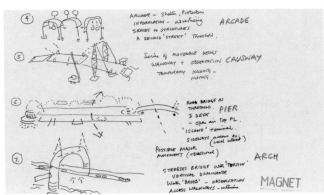

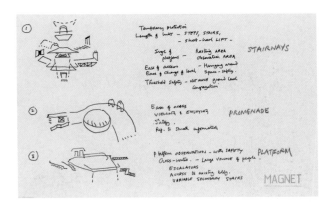

any built environment becomes inhibiting, restrictive, obsolete, unless it can adapt to the yet-to-be-determined. The Fun Palace (1959–61) was the first of such visionary projects, for a site in East London and for theatre director Joan Littlewood. It is not uninteresting to note that much of Kiesler's work was in designing sets and stages such as the Endless Theatre (1925), and culminated in a model for the Universal Theatre (1960–62).

Magnet (1996–99) demonstrates the most recent manifestation of Price's ideas – Greater London is the site, its current and future citizens all potential clients. The scheme takes the form of a series of ten short life structures used to set up new kinds of public amenity or public movement. To be funded by local authorities, and therefore economical to build, Magnets exist for 'the continual necessity of change', turning space to public advantage. Magnets are inherently mobile; the demountable, reusable structures are comprised of such elements as cranes, scissor lifts and airport transporters to be used as bridges, platforms and decks. They provide either better access to a railway station or a view for which one would normally have to pay. Magnet sites are the commonly perceived nonsites such as the air rights above streets, parks and railways. Magnets are designed to make these places more useful, 'more delightful and better fun'.

Price grew up in the 1940s and 1950s with an understanding of the low-tech, the mechanical and the logical, conscious of a common sense. This laid an indestructible foundation for the opening of his offices in 1960, in thinking and speculating about a future that is high-tech, digital, nonlinear, a kind of common non-sense. Although overwhelmingly humanistic in his intent, the affection and contempt that Price holds in equal measures for all technology and some humans is where his unique insight lies. Magnet appeared when the office was almost a sprightly 40 years old and at a time when the political climate was optimistic for all, with a seemingly radical change in government occurring after 18 years of Conservative domination. Price welcomed in the New Labour government with a presentation to them of Magnet as 'a working agenda for change'. The rest is history – or rather we are living it. However, the joy of Magnet is that it could still be built anywhere. The marvellous thing about believing in possibility rather than probability is that the idea will 'benefit from necessary change'. ∆

Note
1. 'Frederick Kiesler 1890–1965', Architectural Association, 1989, exhibition catalogue, advised by Yehuda Safran.
2. Quote from *Cedric Price – Works II*, Architectural Association, 1984, p 47, now *The Square Book*, Wiley Academy, 2003.

Cedric Price, *The Square Book* (paperback, 116 pages, £24.95, ISBN 0470514765) and Samantha Hardingham, *Cedric Price: Opera* (paperback, 128 pages, £24.95, ISBN 0470848758) are available from: John Wiley & Sons Ltd, 1 Oldlands Way, Bognor Regis, West Sussex PO22 9SA, UK. Tel: 0800 243407 (UK freephone) or +44 (0)1243 843303 (from overseas). Fax: +44 (0)1243 843303. Email: cs-books@wiley.co.uk.

Subscribe Now for 2003

As an influential and prestigious architectural publication, *Architectural Design* has an almost unrivalled reputation worldwide. Published bimonthly, it successfully combines the currency and topicality of a newsstand journal with the editorial rigour and design qualities of a book. Consistently at the forefront of cultural thought and design since the 1960s, it has time and again proved provocative and inspirational – inspiring theoretical, creative and technological advances. Prominent in the 1980s for the part it played in Postmodernism and then in Deconstruction, Δ has recently taken a pioneering role in the technological revolution of the 1990s. With groundbreaking titles dealing with cyberspace and hypersurface architecture, it has pursued the conceptual and critical implications of high-end computer software and virtual realities. Δ

Δ Architectural Design

SUBSCRIPTION RATES 2003
Institutional Rate: UK £160
Personal Rate: UK £99
Discount Student* Rate: UK £70
OUTSIDE UK
Institutional Rate: US $240
Personal Rate: US $150
Student* Rate: US $105

*Proof of studentship will be required when placing an order. Prices reflect rates for a 2002 subscription and are subject to change without notice.

TO SUBSCRIBE
Phone your credit card order:
+44 (0)1243 843 828

Fax your credit card order to:
+44 (0)1243 770 432

Email your credit card order to:
cs-journals@wiley.co.uk

Post your credit card or cheque order to:
John Wiley & Sons Ltd.
Journals Administration Department
1 Oldlands Way
Bognor Regis
West Sussex PO22 9SA
UK

Please include your postal delivery address with your order.

All Δ volumes are available individually. To place an order please write to:
John Wiley & Sons Ltd
Customer Services
1 Oldlands Way
Bognor Regis
West Sussex PO22 9SA

Please quote the ISBN number of the issue(s) you are ordering.

Δ is available to purchase on both a subscription basis and as individual volumes

---

○ I wish to subscribe to Δ *Architectural Design* at the **Institutional rate of £160.**

○ I wish to subscribe to Δ *Architectural Design* at the **Personal rate of £99.**

○ I wish to subscribe to Δ *Architectural Design* at the **Student rate of £70.**

STARTING FROM ISSUE 1/2003.

○ Payment enclosed by Cheque/Money order/Drafts.

Value/Currency £/US$ ▢

○ Please charge £/US$ ▢ to my credit card.
Account number:

▢▢▢▢▢▢▢▢▢▢▢▢▢▢▢▢

Expiry date:

▢▢▢▢▢▢

Card: Visa/Amex/Mastercard/Eurocard *(delete as applicable)*

Cardholder's signature ▢

Cardholder's name ▢

Address ▢
▢
▢ Post/Zip Code ▢

Recipient's name ▢

Address ▢
▢
▢ Post/Zip Code ▢

I would like to buy the following issues at £22.50 each:

○ Δ 164 *Home Front: New Developments in Housing*, Lucy Bullivant
○ Δ 163 *Art + Architecture*, Ivan Margolius
○ Δ 162 *Surface Consciousness*, Mark Taylor
○ Δ 161 *Off the Radar*, Brian Carter + Annette LeCuyer
○ Δ 160 *Food + Architecture*, Karen A Franck
○ Δ 159 *Versioning in Architecture*, SHoP
○ Δ 158 *Furniture + Architecture*, Edwin Heathcote
○ Δ 157 *Reflexive Architecture*, Neil Spiller
○ Δ 156 *Poetics in Architecture*, Leon van Schaik
○ Δ 155 *Contemporary Techniques in Architecture*, Ali Rahim
○ Δ 154 *Fame and Architecture*, J. Chance and T. Schmiedeknecht
○ Δ 153 *Looking Back in Envy*, Jan Kaplicky
○ Δ 152 *Green Architecture*, Brian Edwards
○ Δ 151 *New Babylonians*, Iain Borden + Sandy McCreery
○ Δ 150 *Architecture + Animation*, Bob Fear
○ Δ 149 *Young Blood*, Neil Spiller
○ Δ 148 *Fashion and Architecture*, Martin Pawley
○ Δ 147 *The Tragic in Architecture*, Richard Patterson
○ Δ 146 *The Transformable House*, Jonathan Bell and Sally Godwin
○ Δ 145 *Contemporary Processes in Architecture*, Ali Rahim
○ Δ 144 *Space Architecture*, Dr Rachel Armstrong
○ Δ 143 *Architecture and Film II*, Bob Fear
○ Δ 142 *Millennium Architecture*, Maggie Toy and Charles Jencks
○ Δ 141 *Hypersurface Architecture II*, Stephen Perrella
○ Δ 140 *Architecture of the Borderlands*, Teddy Cruz
○ Δ 139 *Minimal Architecture II*, Maggie Toy